THE HERMITAGE
STEP BY STEP

Foreword by Mikhail Piotrovsky

Text by Liudmila Torshina
English translation by Paul Williams
Design by Vasily Bertels

Photographs by Vasily Bertels, Leonid Bogdanov, Leonid Kheifets,
Vladimir Mikhailov, Yury Molodkovets, Victor Savik, Yevgeny Siniaver,
Georgy Skachkov, Svetlana Suyetova, Vladimir Terebenin

Managing Editor: Nina Grishina
Editors: Nina Grishina and Maria Lyzhenkova
Computer typesetting by Nadezhda Lakatosh, Denis Surkov
Colour correction by Yekaterina Shumikhina

ISBN 978-5-902757-62-7

THE HERMITAGE
STEP BY STEP

Alfa-Colour Art Publishers
Saint Petersburg
2013

Johann Baptist Lampi the Elder
Portrait of Empress Catherine II
1793
Oil on canvas

View of Palace Square
and the Winter Palace

THE HERMITAGE is many-sided and all-embracing. It is a cultural treasure-house and guardian of world-ranking masterpieces. Here, as is well known, you can see everything that has been made by humanity in the course of its long history in different parts of the world: masterpieces of European painting by Leonardo da Vinci, Rembrandt, Rubens, Poussin, the Impressionists, Cézanne, Van Gogh, Matisse and Picasso, the gold of the Scythians and Ancient Greeks, Byzantine and Russian icons and Buddhist frescoes, Islamic bronzes and Ancient Roman sculptural portraits, sumptuous Italian majolica and exquisite Chinese porcelain...

The museum with a non-Russian name – a hermitage or "place of seclusion" for Empress Catherine II and for many years now one of the great museums of the world, Russia's main museum is a Russian cultural monument and a symbol of Russia's involvement in world culture. All the history of the Russian Empire took place here: Peter the Great died here; Catherine II ruled the state and founded her museum here. The wind of revolutions passed through its halls, as did the cold and misery of the siege. Its walls retain the grateful memory of those who gathered, preserved and saved its treasures and of the scholars who revealed them to the world.

The Hermitage is also a superb architectural ensemble: nine palace and museum buildings, designed by Russia's finest architects with Russian and foreign names: Rastrelli's Winter palace – the residence of Russian emperors; the exquisite

Small and austere Old Hermitage created by Velten and Vallin de la Mothe; Quarenghi's Hermitage Theatre; the New Hermitage, a masterpiece of museum architecture by Klenze and Stasov; and Rossi's General Staff. There is also the palace of St Petersburg's first governor, Alexander Menshikov, across the Neva, and, in a very different part of the city, Staraya Derevnia, the Restoration and Storage Centre – the latest building of a museum advancing into a new era, a new millennium.

The Hermitage is a museum open to the world in a broad, friendly manner. Thousands of people from all parts of the globe come to see it. How can they avoid becoming lost in this noisy vastness? How can they grasp all its facets? Modern life has made people all but forget what quiet and solitude in a museum is. Perhaps our old friend the book will help us to remember: it will conduct curious visitors through the halls of the great museum and help them to focus on the things that make up its unique character, glory and pride.

MIKHAIL PIOTROVSKY

Director of the State Hermitage
Corresponding Member of the Russian Academy of Sciences
Full Member of the Russian Academy of Arts
Professor of St Petersburg University
Doctor of Historical Sciences

The World of the Hermitage

The Hermitage is huge and many-sided, just like human culture reflected in its collections. It is a microcosm of people's creativity throughout history – from the earliest traces of cultural activity to the work of artists in the century just past. Painting, sculpture, graphic and applied art, coins, weapons, banners, tools and books. The Hermitage's almost three million items in a setting of magnificent buildings form a special world, rich and stirringly beautiful.

It began with the construction of the Winter Palace, the imperial residence, and the addition to it of a small building that Catherine II made her "hermitage" – a secluded retreat of a kind fashionable with the eighteenth-century elite, intended for relaxation and "enlightened" amusements with a select circle of guests. It also became the home for the art works that Catherine began to collect in 1764 with the acquisition of 225 paintings from the Berlin merchant Gotzkowsky. In the almost 250 years since, Catherine's "hermitage" has turned into one of the world's largest museums. The paintings, for which it is still famous, are now only part of it. All the exhibits are divided between seven departments, each of which is a sort of "museum within a museum". Western European art belongs to two departments – fine and applied art. The "keepers of antiquities" are the Departments of the Archaeology of Eastern Europe and Siberia and of the Ancient World. The Department of the East covers cultures and arts from deep antiquity right up, in some cases, to the early twentieth century: Ancient Egypt, Byzantium, the countries of the Middle East and Central Asia, China and India... The Department of the History of Russian Culture concentrates on works connected with

View of the Hermitage

The Winter Palace
The Main Gate. 1880s
Architects: Nikolai Gornostayev,
Roman Melzer

the nation's history, applied art, icons and portraits. The Numismatic Department is the seventh and oldest subdivision of the Hermitage. All of this – the museum's stocks, displays and infrastructure – is housed in an immense complex of nine buildings: seven palaces, a service block and the ultra-modern Repository.

How can you avoid getting lost in that world? How can you go around it, sense its uniqueness and see the best and most important things? This book will be your guide to the world of the Hermitage. It will take you through the museum's main displays, helping you to see and appreciate the beauty of the halls. It will tell you about their creators, about the history of the museum, show you the famous masterpieces and reveal their value and significance.

Our route runs through the main museum ensemble in the centre of St Petersburg – the Winter Palace and the adjoining Small, Old and New Hermitages. The guide also provides information about the separate displays housed in the General Staff building across Palace Square, the Menshikov Palace and other locations.

The wrought-iron gates of the triple-arched grand entrance to the Winter Palace are the main way into the Hermitage. The palace, a masterpiece of Russian Baroque architecture, occupies an immense area between the Neva, whose waves echo the rhythm of the snow-white columns on its northern façade, the Admiralty on the west and vast Palace Square, to which it turns its grandest façade. We pass through the open gates, cross the main courtyard and begin our journey in the world of the Hermitage.

Panorama of Palace Square and the General Staff building

View of the New Hermitage from Millionnaya Street
Watercolour by Luigi Premazzi. 1861

Frans Hals (between 1581 and 1585–1666). Portrait of a Man. Before 1660
Oil on canvas. Acquired as part of the Gotzkowsky collection

< View of Palace Embankment by the Winter Palace and the Hermitage from the Spit of Vasilyevsky Island in St Petersburg
Watercolour by B. Paterssen 1799

The Winter Palace

The Main Gallery. 1754–62;
1837–39
Architects: Francesco Bartolomeo
Rastrelli; Vasily Stasov

The Main Staircase. Sculpture:
Justice. Detail. Early 18th century
Sculptor: Alvise Tagliapetra. Italy
Marble. Height 202 cm

Lucas Conrad Pfandzelt
Portrait of the Architect
Francesco Bartolomeo Rastrelli
1750s – 1760s
Oil on canvas

Louis Tocqué (1696–1772)
Portrait of Empress
Elizabeth (1709–1761) 1758
Oil on canvas. 262 x 204 cm
(Hall 151)

Ascending ramps that were originally made for carriages, you enter the vestibule of the Winter Palace, containing ticket windows, an information desk and cloakrooms. From it you move into a spacious, three-aisled gallery decorated with sculpture and stone vases, its tall vaults resting on mighty piers, that leads to the Main Staircase. Its lower flight soon becomes visible as does the gold-framed niche above, containing an allegorical statue of Justice, whose residence the Winter Palace once was. This is the last in a series of imperial winter residences that were built on this bank of the River Neva after the foundation of St Petersburg as the new capital of the Russian Empire. After the death of the city's founder, Peter the Great (reigned 1682–1725), his small palace between the Neva and the Winter Canal fell into decay and when Anna Ioannovna (r. 1730–1740) came to the throne, she occupied the mansion of Admiral General Apraxin, the best of the palaces from Peter's time that stood on the same embankment. Although reconstructed and enlarged,

8

it was deemed unworthy of "the greatness of the imperial dignity" in the reign of Empress Elizabeth (r. 1741–1761), when Russia's power and autocracy had grown. So between 1752 and 1762 the architect Francesco Bartolomeo Rastrelli (1700–1771) erected a new Winter Palace. Rastrelli was not permitted to complete the project, however: the majority of the interiors were created after his dismissal, which followed the enthronement of a new ruler – Catherine II (r. 1762–1796). Still the grandeur of his brilliant conception was perpetuated in the palace's exterior.

One of the few interiors that Rastrelli did design was the Main Staircase. It was intended as a grand entrance that would astonish guests with its sumptuous magnificence. Ascending the first flight of stairs, we emerge from the shady vaults and immediately enter a boundless, dazzlingly bright space. Light floods in through two rows of windows; it is reflected in mirrors and scatters in pearly patches, slipping across the walls, statues and vases, the gilded mouldings, the marble floors, steps and balustrades... The walls, enlivened by light, a dynamic rhythm of single and paired columns, gilded cornices, branched candelabra and ornaments, do not seem to be a barrier enclosing the space, but a living "breathing" surface that opens to the outside beyond the windows, where the Neva's waves lap beneath the St Petersburg sky. At the unreachable height of 22 metres the gods of Olympus hover in the blue heaven of a ceiling painting by the eighteenth-century Venetian artist Gasparo Diziani. From pedestals sup-

The Main (Jordan) Staircase
The twin flights (Hall 1)

The Main Staircase
Watercolour by Konstantin Ukhtomsky
1860s. 44,2 × 31,3

ported by caryatids statues of gods and muses made in Italy and Russia look down, allegorically extolling the might and wisdom of the rulers. And all this splendour is united by the soaring ascent of the white marble stairs that separate into two broad flights at the lower landing. Pausing for a moment at the middle landings, they meet again at the first floor and the ten granite columns that frame the upper landing take over the up-ward movement, climbing to the sky and the light. Although the granite of the columns and the marble of the balustrades came later, in the nineteenth cen-tury, the Main Staircase remains a superb example of the sumptuous, festive, life-affirming style of the Russian Baroque, whose finest architect was Rastrelli.

From the upper landing you can enter both the Neva and Great Enfilades of state rooms. We shall go to the Field Marshals' Hall that begins the Great Enfilade.

The Main Staircase
Upper landing

The Main Staircase
1754–62; 1837–39
Architects: Francesco Bartolomeo
Rastrelli; Vasily Stasov

The Main Staircase
Ceiling painting: Olympus
1750s. Italy
Painter: Gasparo Diziani

The Main Staircase
Caryatid

What a contrast between the rather austere restraint of the Field Marshals' Hall and the festive spirit of the Baroque staircase we just left. It is easy to grasp its rectangular plan. Ionic porticos around the entrances and pilasters along the walls support a classical entablature: a smooth architrave, ornamental frieze and cornice with carved consoles and a marble balustrade above. The walls are divided into equal areas by the door and window openings alternating with shallow niches that once contained the portraits of Russian field marshals that gave the hall its name. The paintings were removed after the 1917 revolution, but the depictions of Suvorov, Kutuzov and Paskevich have now returned to their places. The images of great commanders and trophies – compositions of arms and armour – in the moulding, decorative painting and chandeliers (whose gilded bronze enlivens the coldness of the pearly-grey colour scheme) give the hall an austere military character: this was the place where the elite palace guard kept watch and was changed. The strictness of the architecture – the use of a classical order, symmetry and sparing use of decoration – are all features of Classicism that was the prevailing style in the early decades of the nineteenth century. The hall was the work of two great exponents of that style. It was created in 1833–34 by Auguste de Montferrand (1786–1858), but the great fire that raged through the palace in December 1837 destroyed all its interiors. The restoration of the imperial residence was directed by the outstanding Late Classical architect Vasily Stasov (1769–1848), who became the second father of the Field Marshals' Hall, recreating it almost entirely to Montferrand's design.

The Field Marshals' Hall
1833; 1838–39
Architects: Auguste Montferrand;
Vasily Stasov (Hall 193)

The Field Marshals' Hall. Detail

The Field Marshals' Hall
Watercolour by Eduard Hau. 1866
33.1 x 42.6 cm

11

The Peter the breat Hall
(Small Throne Room) Detail:
the ceiling painting and the silver
chandelier

The Peter the breat Hall
(Small Throne Room).
Detail of lunette painting.
1838–39
Artists: Barnaba Medici, Pietro Scotti

The Peter the Great Hall
1833; 1838–39
Architects: Auguste Montferrand;
Vasily Stasov
(Hall 194)

V asily Stasov also recreated Montferrand's design for the following room almost without
modification. The Peter the Great Hall was
made at the same time as the Field Marshals' Hall
"with great haste", which may have indirectly been
the cause of the fire in 1837: unused building materials and rags left behind by the workmen in a wall
cavity were set alight by sparks from a slowly smoul-
dering fire between the walls of the Field Marshals'
and Peter the Great Halls that had its ultimate source
in the constantly stoked stoves of the palace phar-
macy located on the ground floor below. The palace
staff were unable to track down the fire for a long
time, and before they managed to do so, the flames
from the burning wall cavity sprang over onto the
tar-impregnated rafters and the whole vast area of
the palace ceilings was instantly alight. The blaze
became unstoppable.

It is not clear whether Montferrand was actually
responsible for the disaster, but after the fire the celebrated architect of St Isaac's Cathedral was dis-
charged from work on the Winter Palace. Still, Stasov
had a profound understanding of his predecessor's
concept and style. This hall was conceived as a memorial to Peter the Great, the founder of the Russian
Empire. Stasov repeated Montferrand's composition
of a rectangular space with, as a focal point, a semicircular niche in the centre of the long wall opposite
the windows. The side walls "lead" to this niche.
They are lined with crimson Lyons velvet bearing
bronze double-headed eagles and Peter's monogram – two Latin letter Ps, standing for Petrus
Primus (Peter the First).
The monogram and Russian coat-of-arms can be seen
everywhere here: at the base of the walls, in the moulded capitals and frieze and in the ceiling painting.
Placed on the upper part of both side walls, facing

Jacopo Amiconi. 1675–1752
Peter the Great with the Goddess
of Wisdom Minerva
Between 1732 and 1735
Oil on canvas. 231x178 cm

The Peter Hall (Small Throne
Room) Detail of the niche with
the imperial crown and the
monogram of Peter the Great

each other, are two paintings depicting famous victories in the Great Northern War (1700–21) in which Peter fought against Sweden to gain access to the Baltic Sea: the Battles of Poltava and Lesnaya. Paired pilasters spaced evenly along the walls give way to a group of columns supporting the arch above the niche that is designed like the sanctuary of a Russian Orthodox church. Within it, on a marble pedestal beneath a richly ornamented cornice that is topped by an imperial crown, is a painting framed by columns of wavy green jasper in which the first Russian emperor is shown with his loyal companion – Minerva, the Ancient Roman goddess of wisdom and war. The image was produced by the Italian painter Jacopo Amigoni after Peter's death to a commission from Prince Antioch Cantemir, Russia's ambassador to Britain who was also a satirical poet and one of the most educated men of his time. The artist used a portrait painted by the French artist Louis Caravaque in the Tsar's lifetime as the basis for the creation of a striking allegory, extolling the Emperor's wisdom and military genius. The throne, upholstered in velvet with a double-headed eagle on the back and a crown above it, was made in 1737 for Empress Anna Ioannovna by the craftsman N. Clausen. Silver chandeliers, tables and candelabra and a parquet floor made up of precious varieties of wood complete this sumptuous interior. The Peter the Great Hall is also known as the Small Throne-Room.

Sergei Zarianko. 1817–1870
The Peter Hall
(Small Throne Room) 1836
Oil on canvas. 86 x 109.5cm

The Armorial Hall. 1838–39
Architect: Vasily Stasov (Hall 195)

Adolphe Ladurner. 1798–1855
View of the White (Armorial)
Hall in the Winter Palace. 1838
Oil on canvas. 69 x 96 cm

The Armorial Hall. Chandelier
1838–39
Architects: Vasily Stasov, Vladimir
Schreiber. Gilded metal composition

We emerge from the memorial Peter the Great Hall, a colourful "temple" rich in decorative forms, but relatively small in size, into the huge Armorial Hall glistening with gold and cold official solemnity. It was a tradition for formal residences that one of the halls should be decorated with the coat-of-arms of the ruler's territories. The arms of the various provinces making up the Russian Empire are depicted here on small bronze shields attached to the great chandeliers. In this hall the emperor would receive delegations from the provincial centres of the country and representatives of the different estates – the local nobility, municipal heads and the merchants.

The interior was designed by Vasily Stasov. The architect enlarged the hall that had existed here before the 1837 fire, turning it into the second-largest in the palace with a floor area of about 1,000 square metres. He employed the typical Classical composition of the columned hall: a majestic colonnade of fully gilded Corinthian columns runs around the perimeter of the hall, underlining the

14

strict regularity of its rectangular plan. The paired columns, rhythmically alternating with the arched window embrasures support an entablature with a frieze richly ornamented with gilded bronze. Above it, on the corbels of the strongly projecting cornice, runs a massive balustrade enclosing the gallery. Stasov did not only use such galleries as a decorative element to adorn the main state rooms, he also intended them to have a potential fire-fighting function, that being one of the architect's tasks when reconstructing the Winter Palace after the catastrophe.

By the end walls of the hall, either side of the entrance porticos, stand sculptural groups of old Russian warriors with banners and heraldic symbols. These sculptures repeat the compositions that existed here before the fire and once bore the armorial shields that were then transferred to the chandeliers, forming a thread that links Stasov's interior with the historical past.

History is always alive in the walls of the Hermitage. The Armorial Hall preserves many memories. One of the most tragic of those memories dates from the time of the 900-day Siege of Leningrad (1941–44). Of the twenty-two shells that hit the Hermitage buildings one fell here. It pierced the inside wall of the Armorial Hall and the floor just by the entrance to the Peter the Great Hall: the blast dislodged the bronze chandelier there, which fell and wrecked the parquet floor. After the war a similar chandelier from the museum stocks was used as a replacement, the floors and walls were restored, but the echoes of history are not forgotten.

The Armorial Hall. Detail
(Hall 195)

The Armorial Hall. Sculptural group of Russian warriors.
1829–31; 1840
Sculptors: Vasily Demuth-Malinovsky, N. Tokarev (from a drawing by Carlo Rossi); A. Streichenberg

The Armorial Hall
Detail of the frieze and balustrade of the balcony

George Dawe. 1781–1829
Portrait of Denis Davydov
No later than 1828
Oil on canvas. 70 x 62.5 cm (Hall 197)

Franz von Krüger. 1797–1857
Equestrian Portrait of Emperor
Alexander I. 1837
Oil on canvas. 484 x 344 cm (Hall 197)

George Dawe. 1781–1829
Portrait of Prince Piotr Bagration
Circa 1823
Oil on canvas. 70 x 62.5 cm (Hall 197)

Russia's heroic history finds expression in one of the most famous interiors of the Great Enfilade of state rooms. This is the Gallery of 1812, a monument in architecture and paints to the country's victory in the titanic struggle against Napoleon's invasion, a monument to the great feat of the Russian army that saved the country and went on to liberate Europe from the French Emperor's deadly embrace.

The gallery was constructed soon after the end of the war, consecrated and formally inaugurated on 25 December 1826, the day when Russia each year commemorated the anniversary of the invading army being driven out of the country. Its creation was the work of the architect Carlo Rossi (1775–1849) and the English portrait-painter George Dawe (1781–1829). Dawe painted British participants of the Napoleonic wars for a memorial hall at Windsor Castle, the royal residence outside London. After seeing these during his visit to England, Alexander I decided to create a similar memorial in his own Winter Palace.

Dawe was invited to Russia and a studio was created for him and his two Russian assistants Alexander Poliakov and Vasily (Wilhelm) Golicke, to which on the Emperor's orders generals who had fought in the "Patriotic War" came to pose for the artist. In all 332 portraits were painted; some – of officers who had died on the battlefield – were produced on the basis of depictions made in their lifetimes. Yet despite all such efforts, when the portraits were installed, thirteen frames had to be left empty, lined with green

16

George Dawe. 1781–1829
Portrait of Prince
Mikhail Kutuzov. 1829
Oil on canvas. 361 x 268 cm (Hall 197)

silk, to preserve the memory of those whose appearance remained unknown. And so from the walls of the gallery arranged in five rows of identical frames, there look out at us stern courageous warriors wearing epaulets, the stars and sashes of orders of chivalry– "all capes and sabres and faces full of martial valour", as the great Russian poet Alexander Pushkin put it. These are the upper echelons of the army that defeated the invincible Bonaparte.

All the portraits were carried from the gallery during the 1837 fire by soldiers of the palace grenadiers company, themselves veterans of the 1812 war, and this enabled Stasov to restore the gallery to Rossi's design. Dawe's portraits of some of the grenadiers also hang in the gallery that they saved. The rows of chest-length portraits are separated by full-length depictions of the commanders-in-chief of the Russian and allied armies. On the end wall is an equestrian portrait of Emperor Alexander I; at his sides are King Frederick William III of Prussia and Emperor Francis I of Austria. In the places of greatest honour, flanking the entrance to the Large Throne Room, are the likenesses of the men who commanded the Russian army – Field Marshals Mikhail Barclay de Tolly and Mikhail Kutuzov.

The Gallery of 1812
1826; 1838–39
Architects: Carlo Rossi; Vasily Stasov
(Hall 197)

< George Dawe 1781–1829
Portrait of Prince
Nikolai Rayevsky. Circa 1825
Oil on canvas. 70 x 62.5 cm (Hall 197)

17

The Great Church of the Winter Palace. 1754–62; 1838–39
Architects: Francesco Bartolomeo Rastrelli; Vasily Stasov
(Halls 270, 271)

The Great Church
The moulded and gilded cartouche with the monogram of Empress Elizabeth

The Great Church
Pendentive depicting the Evangelist Matthew

> The Great Church. 1860
Watercolour by Eduard Hau. 1860
45.5 x 34.5 см

The exit at the opposite end of the Gallery of 1812 to the portrait of Alexander I leads to a small area that links the state rooms to what was once the residential part of the palace: the gallery is behind us; to the right is the Picket Hall ("picket" in the sense of a unit of the palace guard); ahead are rooms that belonged to the reserve (guest) apartments and now house the display of French art; while to the left are the wide-open doors of the glittering Great Church of the Winter Palace.

The large space that seems to suddenly open outwards and upwards, the light and air entering through two tiers of high windows and from beneath the dome that soars away from us, the rapid, whimsical scurry of the gilded ornament on the walls, arches, cornices and vaults – all of this inevitably recalls to mind the Main Staircase by which we entered the palace not long ago. These are indeed the same architectural devices, the same exultant, festive Baroque style. The Great Church was the second interior that Francesco Bartolomeo Rastrelli, the builder of the Winter Palace, managed to finish before his dismissal. In Rastrelli's concept the church was an important part of the imperial apartments, which in the eighteenth century were located in

the south-eastern part of the palace – where French art is now on show. These were the private quarters of the first mistress of the Winter Palace – Empress Catherine II. From there she entered the church directly through the sacristy and after the services the grand processions that were a key element of court ceremonial began directly from the church.

Consecrated at the end of construction in 1762 in the name of the Resurrection, the Great Church was reconsecrated in 1763, on Catherine's orders almost immediately after she took the throne, in honour of the holy image known as the Vernicle. When the church was restored after the 1837 fire, two professors from the St Petersburg Academy of Arts, Fiodor Bruni and Piotr Basin, recreated the Baroque painting of the eighteenth-century Italian artist Francesco Fontebasso: the figures of the four Evangelists on the pendentives (the curved triangles below the dome) and the Resurrection on the ceiling.

The Great Church belonged to the state rooms of the palace: all official ceremonies in the imperial residence began with a church service. Although at the present time the Great Church is used for temporary exhibitions of icons and other works of Christian art, it remains a very important element in the Great Enfilade of state rooms, lying directly alongside its most important hall – the Large Throne Room. Let us return to the Gallery of 1812, as guests at the palace would once have done, and enter the Large Throne Room.

Dome of the Great Church with representations of the four Evangelists on the pendentives 1838–39
Artists: Fiodor Bruni, Piotr Basin

Immediately after the restoration of the Winter Palace following the 1837 fire, Nicholas I gave orders for the appearance of its halls and buildings to be recorded in watercolours and drawings. Thus, thanks to the work of talented artists of the middle and second half of the nineteenth century, we have a priceless pictorial record of the architecture and life of the imperial residence.

The Large Throne Room
(St George Hall)
1838–41. Architect: Vasily Stasov
(Hall 198)

The Large Throne Room
Relief representation
of St George over the throne dais.
1842–44
Sculptor: Francesco del Nero. Marble

The grand splendour of the chief hall of the Winter Palace reveals itself from the heavy entrance doors. Gleaming with white Carrara marble set off by gilded bronze, rows of columns and stone vases, a smooth frieze, cornice and balustrade above lead the eye to the throne dais. There, on a platform covered with crimson velvet beneath a sumptuous canopy and in front of a panel bearing the coat-of-arms of the Russian Empire stands the Great Imperial Throne. This grand chair of gilded silver on a wooden base, upholstered in velvet with a double-headed eagle on the back and a crown above it is a copy of the throne that was made in England for Empress Anna Ioannovna in the 1730s. This copy was made for Emperor Paul I by Meyer in St Petersburg in 1797. The immense space of this hall – with a floor area of 800 square metres the third largest in the palace – is transfused with light. Two rows of windows, between the columns and above, run along each side of the hall. It occupies two storeys of a separate wing that was built between the projecting blocks of the palace's eastern façade in the late eighteenth century to the design of Giacomo Quarenghi (1744–1817), whom Catherine entrusted with the creation of a new throne room.

Formally inaugurated on 26 November 1795, the Orthodox feast of St George, the patron saint

The opening of the St George's Day celebrations in the St George Hall. 2003

of Russia, Quarenghi's throne room perished in the fire of 1837. While retaining the floor plan and dimensions of the hall, Stasov decorated it in a new way, producing his own finest work. He achieved a harmonious unity between all the decorative and constructional elements. The immense ceiling is held up by a complex arrangement of metal girders first employed in the 1830s. The copper plates attached to it were decorated with splendid gilded bronze ornament. The same pattern is mirrored in the parquet floor in which sixteen precious varieties of wood were used. On the wall above the throne dais is a bas-relief by the Italian sculptor Del Niro depicting St George, the Bringer of Victory.

The St George Hall or Large Throne Room of the Winter Palace is a masterpiece of nineteenth-century Russian Classicism, the pride of the nation's architecture. It was and still is the setting for significant events. In tsarist times the most important state ceremonies took place here; today it is used for the State Hermitage's grandest events. The fates of the Winter Palace and the museum are inseparable. From the St George Hall we take the doors on either side of the throne dais to enter the building with which the history of the Hermitage began.

The Large Throne Room
(St George Hall)

Nicholas II's speech from the throne in the St George Hall marked the formal opening of Russia's first Duma (parliament)
Photo. 1906

The Large Throne Room
(St George Hall). The throne dais.
Throne. 1797. Russia
By Ch. Meyer (copy of the throne of Empress Anna Ioannovna). Wood, velvet, silver-gilt. 183 x 87 x 104 cm

21

The Small Hermitage

The Small Hermitage
The Northern Pavilion. 1767–69
Architect: Jean-Baptiste
Vallin de la Mothe

Vigilius Erichsen. Portrait of
Catherine the Great before a
Mirror. Between 1762 and 1764
Oil on canvas. 262,5 x 201,5

Carl Ludwig Johann Christineck
Portrait of the Architect
Yury Velten. 1770s
Oil on canvas

The Hanging Garden
18th-century marble fountain
and decorative sculpture

P assing through the adjoining Apollo Hall, we come out in the middle of a long gallery. We have left the Winter Palace and are now in the Small Hermitage. Beyond the windows lies a garden at second-storey level, the famous Hanging Garden of Catherine II, the "Semiramis of the North". Across the garden, the Eastern Gallery runs parallel to this Western one. At the end of the garden to the right is the Southern Pavilion, which when first built provided accommodation for Catherine II's favourites close to her own; to the left the Northern Pavilion, originally also known as the La Mothe Pavilion after Jean-Baptiste Vallin de la Mothe (1729–1800), who designed this elegant building and its fine Classical façade overlooking the Neva.

Altogether these elements make up the Small Hermitage, the smallest building in the presend-day museum ensemble, constructed in 1764–75 under the direction of the outstanding architect Yury Velten (1730–1801).

The he northern part of the Western Gallery contains a display of mediaeval applied art dating from between the years 500 and 1500. This was the time of the emergence of European civilization after the fall of the Roman Empire. It was the age of knights and crusades, castles and churches, bloody feudal strife and chivalrous courtly love, the time of Europe's youth. Its spiritual and ideological foundation was Christianity. The monasteries of the Romanesque period were the first seats of mediaeval culture; the grand urban Gothic cathedrals great artistic achievements. Church utensils and items of everyday use from feudal castles and courts – the statuettes of the Virgin and carved ivory ornaments, items of precious metal, tapestries and ceramics on display – give a vivid picture of the work of mediaeval craftsmen.

Find in one of the cases an aquamanile (water-jug) in the form of a knight fighting a dragon. This is one of the masterpieces of the collection of artistic bronzes, an allegory of the struggle between Good and Evil. The Hermitage's collection of Limoges enamels is widely known (that French city was one of the main centres of enamel-making in the Middle Ages). Particularly celebrated is a twelfth-century reliquary bearing scenes from the life of St Valeria, an early martyr and patron saint of Aquitaine. This casket was created on the occasion of the mystic betrothal of the saint and the Duke of Aquitaine, later King Richard the Lion-Heart of England, that took place in 1170.

The Western Gallery. Display of mediaeval Western European applied art (Hall 259)

Reliquary with scenes from the life of Saint Valeria Late 12th century Limoges, France
Copper with champlevé enamel and wood. Height: 19.5 cm; length: 27.7 cm; width: 11.7 cm (Hall 259)

Aquamanile in the shape of a knight fighting a dragon 13th century. Western Europe
Bronze. Height 18.5 cm, length 30 cm (Hall 259)

Plaques bearing scenes from the romance of Tristan and Isolde. Germany(?). Mid-14th century
Carved ivory. 8.2 x 18.5 x 10 cm (Hall 259)

> Lucas van Leyden
(1489 or 1494–1533).
The Healing of the
Blind Man of Jericho.
Triptych. 1531
Oil on canvas, transferred
from panel
Central composition:
115.5 x 150.5 cm;
side panels: 89 x 33.5 cm
(Hall 262)

Jan Provost
(circa 1465–1529)
The Virgin in Glory. 1524
Oil on canvas, transferred from panel
203 x 151 cm (Hall 262)

The Western Gallery. in the Small
Hermitage. The Display of 15th–
16th Centuries Netherlandish
Painting (Hall 259)

Robert Campin
(circa 1380–1444)
The Trinity. Virgin and Child at
the Fireplace. 1430s. Diptych
Oil on panel. Each panel: 34 x 24.5 cm
(Hall 261)

The southern part of the gallery contains six-
teenth- and seventeenth-century paintings
from the Low Countries, the birthplace
of easel painting. The relatively small collection
(around 100 works) presents the 200-year history
of one of the earliest and most significant schools
of Western European painting.

Its most valuable item is a small altarpiece by
Robert Campin, the founder of the Netherlandish
school, depicting the Holy Trinity on the left and
the Virgin and Child on the right. The softly lit
scene set in a burgher house conveys an enchanting
sense of warmth and the beauty of earthly existence.
Another acknowledged masterpiece is *St Luke Painting the Virgin* by Rogier van der Weyden, one of the
fifteenth century's greatest artists. The reverent attention in the face of St Luke reflects the delight

and awe of a painter discovering and recording the precious beauty of the world around him. The works of sixteenth-century artists are more monumental and display the influence of the Italian Renaissance. Among the exhibits from this period a special place is occupied by the three-part altar piece *The Healing of the Blind Man of Jericho*. This festive spectacle of one of Christ's miracles against a background of luxuriant greenery, blue mountains and city walls is one of the best works by Lucas van Leyden, created for the Leyden municipal hospital to a commission from local dignitaries, whose arms are displayed by the heralds depicted on the side panels.

This gallery has given us our first encounter with the Hermitage's collections of art. In order to get an idea of the circumstances under which those collections began to form, we need to go to the Northern Pavilion of the Small Hermitage.

Master of the Female Half-Lengths (the conventional designation for an unknown Netherlandish painter who probably worked in Antwerp in the 1530s and 1540s) Female Musicians
Oil on panel. 53 x 37.5 cm *Hall 262*

Exquisite musicians perform the music written (not entirely accurately) in the book in front of them. Their tender looks reflect the ideal of female beauty prevailing in the sixteenth-century Netherlands.

Rogier van der Weyden (circa 1400–1464) St Luke Painting the Virgin. 1430s Oil on canvas, transferred from panel. 102.5 x 108.5 cm (Hall 261)

The Pavilion Hall. 1850–58
Architect: Andrei Stakenschneider
(Hall 204)

The Pavilion Hall. Arcades with
marble Corinthian columns

> View of the central part of the
Pavilion Hall and the Peacock
Clock

The two storeys of the Northern Pavilion are occupied by the single, grand Pavilion Hall. It has
windows on all sides: facing the Neva, the Hanging Garden and the adjoining buildings. At any time
of year light pours into this hall. It passes through the
openwork arcades that run lightly across the hall,
pierces into the corners and beneath the vaults and,
refracting in the crystal of the chandeliers, scatters
across the floor, the walls and the columns of white
Carrara marble.

The bright airy hall is an embodiment of the imagination, taste and erudition of Andrei Stakenscheider
(1802–1865), a master of the eclectic approach. Har-
moniously combining motifs from Classical and Eastern architecture, he produced an exquisite interior.
Arcades in Italian Renaissance style, statues in niches
and columns in the spirit of the Ancient World coex-
ist naturally with reproductions of the famous "Fountain of Tears" in the Islamic palace of Bakhchiserai in
the Crimea. The lacework of Classical mouldings on
the friezes, arches and walls is complemented by the
Moresque pattern of the balcony railings. A copy of a
mosaic from ancient Ocriculum near Rome (excavated in 1780) depicting the Gorgon Medusa and sea
deities is set in the floor where the Orangery was in
the eighteenth century. The arcades stand where once
there were walls dividing the pavilion into six rooms:
the Orangery and adjoining large hall with windows

26

The Peacock Clock
Second half of the 18th century.
James Cox, England
Wood, gilded bronze, silver foil
(Hall 204)

overlooking the Neva, plus four corner cabinets. This was Catherine II's Hermitage. Here in a relaxed atmosphere she held gatherings that usually ended in dinner without servants: the tables were laid below and then raised to the cabinet in the north-east corner. The name "Hermitage" was soon being applied to the art collections kept here. Beginning with an almost chance acquisition – paintings owned by Gotzkowsky in settlement of the merchant's debt to Russia – Catherine quickly built one of Europe's largest art collections. Her consultants and agents were outstanding connoisseurs – the writer and philosopher Denis Diderot, the diplomat Prince Dmitry Golitsyn, the sculptor Etienne Maurice Falconet and the archaeologist Riefenstein.

The Pavilion Hall contains one of Catherine's acquisitions – the Peacock Clock made by the eighteenth-century English craftsman James Cox. The dial is in the cap of the mushroom. When the clock strikes, the cock crows, the owl's cage rotates and the bells on it ring, the peacock spreads its tail and turns slowly. As the collections grew, Catherine ordered the construction of further premises: the Small Hermitage galleries, the Old Hermitage, the Raphael Loggias and the Hermitage Theatre. In the nineteenth century one more building was added to Catherine's Hermitage – the New Hermitage towards which we now head.

The Council Staircase. 1850–56
Architect: Andrei Stakenschneider
(Hall 206)

We have come out onto the upper landing of the Council Staircase. It is a sort of hub for the whole Hermitage ensemble: behind are the Small Hermitage and Winter Palace; straight ahead the Old Hermitage; to the right the New Hermitage, to the ground floor of which we now descend.

The New Hermitage

The New Hermitage
Façade on Millionnaya Street.
1842–51
Architect: Leo von Klenze, with
Vasily Stasov and Nikolai Yefimov

Franz von Krüger. Portrait
of Emperor Nicholas I. 1850s
Oil on canvas

The Gallery of the History
of Ancient Painting. Moulded
medallion with a depiction
of the architect Leo von Klenze

From the Council Staircase we enter the Twenty-Column Hall of the New Hermitage, a building constructed in 1842–51 on the orders of Emperor Nicholas I. The design was the work of the Bavarian architect Leo von Klenze (1784–1864), who had built the Pinakothek and Glyptothek in Munich, but construction was supervised by the architect Vasily Stasov, who reconciled Klenze's project with the existing Hermitage buildings. The New Hermitage occupied a site between the Winter Canal and the Small Hermitage, its "back" to the Old Hermitage and its face to quiet Millionnaya Street on the south.

The building is in the "Neo-Grecian" style. Its entrance takes the form of a majestic portico with granite atlantes (pillars in human form); the interiors are finished in imitation of Ancient Greek architecture.

The Twenty-Column Hall was built like a Greek temple: Ionic columns dividing it into three long aisles, a mosaic floor and a coffered ceiling (with sunken panels) painted with Grecian ornament. On the walls are twelve compositions copied from Grecian vases: this hall was intended for the display of Greco-Etruscan vases. Etruscan vases are still kept in this hall today. Particularly interesting are the vessels made in the *bucchero* technique imitating metal.

The Etruscans lived in central Italy in the eighth to fifth centuries B.C. before their homeland was conquered by the Romans. Their art that has come down to us testifies to a distinct vibrant cul-

ture and contains much that remains a mystery. In the Twenty-Column Hall you can also see examples of the famous Etruscan bronzes. The most outstanding is the lid of a funerary urn decorated with the figure of a reclining youth. The expressive shape of the powerful young torso and the firm gesture of the hand that once held a cup form a strange contrast with the flattening of forms in the lower part of the figure that seem to disappear beneath the folds of the cloak and the immobility of the face and eyes (they would have been coloured, but the lost insets can hardly have enlivened them much). This all creates a mystery. The feast that the youth is attending is not the feast of life, but a sacred ritual, a symbol of the power of death over transient life.

A very different, life-affirming character invests the scene of rites dedicated to Demeter, the goddess of agriculture, in a relief frieze on the shoulders of the famous "Queen of Vases" in the central part of the hall. This finely proportioned black-figure

The Twenby-Column Hall
Architect Leo von Klenze
(Hall 130)

The Twenty-Column Hall
Wall painting of Triptolemus,
Demeter and Persephone (Hall 130)

Reclining Youth. Funerary urn
Etruria. Circa 350 B.C.
Bronze. Height: 42 cm (Hall 130)

Hydria bearing scenes
from the Eleusinian mysteries
(The Queen of Vases). Campagna,
4th century B.C.
Painted earthenware with reliefs.
Height: 62.2 cm (Hall 130)

Crater: Gigantomachy
Lycurgus (craftsman).
Apulia 4th century B.C.
Painted earthenware
Height: 105 cm (Hall 130)

The Kolyvan Vase.
Kolyvan Lapidary Works,
Altai, Russia. 1847
Revnev jasper. Height: 2.5 m;
width: 4.5 m (Hall 128)

The Pompeian Hall
The Display of Ancient Roman
Applied Art of the 1st to 3rd
Centuries (Hall 129)

hydria (water vessel) with a high neck enclosed by lacework and a belt of superbly moulded figures of lions and griffons on its body was found in a rich grave near the city of Cumae in south Italy. It entered the Hermitage as part of the Campana collection, the acquisition of which in 1861 greatly enhanced the Hermitage's ancient stocks. Today the Department of the Ancient World has over 100,000 works of art from Greece, Italy and the cities of the northern Black Sea, covering the whole history of Antiquity from the third millennium B.C. to the fourth century A.D. The Twenty-Column Hall holds only a small portion of the collection of ancient pottery (over 15,000 vases) – Italian ceramics: monumental krater vases that served as grave monuments and pottery in Karelian birch display cases made to Klenze's designs. This display is part of the section devoted to the culture and art of Ancient Italy and Rome.

In the next hall Klenze's shapely pyramids contain small Roman bronzes. To the left of that hall are examples of Ancient Roman glass. But the largest area is taken by Ancient Roman marble sculpture. In order to reach it we pass through a hall containing the famous Kolyvan Vase. This is one of the largest vases in the world, a masterpiece made from Revnev jasper at the Kolyvan Lapidary Works in the Altai. It weighs 19 tonnes, but you do not feel that thanks to the finely struck proportions between its component parts: the huge oval bowl rests lightly on an exquisite stem that stands firmly on the monolithic pedestal.

Passing steps that lead to a passageway between buildings, we reach a spacious hall. A soft light enters through the windows and the pale green of the walls sets off the white of the ancient marbles. They are arranged freely between the pillars making them convenient to view – the architecture here was intended for the display of sculpture in the round. The moulding in the vaults includes relief portraits of great sculptors (of the modern, rather than ancient era, admittedly), since Klenze created this hall for nineteenth-century sculpture. That had to be moved upstairs when almost 100 sculptures arrived in the Campana collection, including a colossal statue of Jupiter, over three metres tall and almost 16 tonnes in weight.

Since then the hall has borne the name of the king of the gods. Jupiter is depicted seated on a throne. A majestic pose, the mature beauty of a powerful athletic body, the dispassionate face and the symbols of power – the eagle, sceptre and the goddess of victory in his hand – Jupiter is the very embodiment of world domination, of the might of the Roman Empire, whose supreme god he was. This statue stood in the temple at the villa of Emperor Domitian (81–96 A.D.). It is a copy of the famous statue of Olympian Zeus created in gold and ivory by the great Greek sculptor Phidias in the fifth century B.C. The Roman sculptor used marble and gilded bronze (lost and replaced by tinted plaster during restoration).

Warriors, builders and law-makers, in art the Romans were the pupils of the Greeks. Almost all

The Hall of Jupiter. The Display of Sculpture from Imperial Rome, 1st to 4th Century (Hall 107)

Statue of Jupiter. Rome
Second half of the 1st century A.D.
Marble and coloured plaster of Paris
Height: 310 cm (Hall 107)

Portrait of a Roman
About mid-3rd century A.D.
Ancient Rome
Marble (Hall 107)

Portrait of Emperor Balbinus
Second quarter
of the 3rd century A.D.
Marble. Height: 72.5 cm (Hall 107)

Bust: Portrait of Emperor Philip I
the Arabian
About mid-3rd century A.D.
Ancient Rome
Marble. Height 72.3 cm (Hall 107)

their monumental sculpture, especially religious art, repeated Greek works. But Roman portraiture was not derivative and became the highest form of plastic art.

The Hermitage has almost 120 Roman sculptural portraits, a collection of world importance. Sculptors began to combine a realistic depiction of appearance that went back to the ancient tradition of death masks with accurate and profound presentation of character and the model's psychological state. Polished marble and the fine modelling of the face framed by an exuberant hairstyle worked in relief and a carefully combed beard, plus a toga fastened by a clasp at the shoulder all indicate a high-born patrician in the portrait of an unknown Roman. He bears some resemblance to Marcus Aurelius's co-ruler Lucius Verus, whose bust stands nearby – the same sort of noble "dandy" from

Rome's gilded youth. But here the sculptor has managed to convey more: cold arrogance, satiation, the inner emptiness of a ruler from the time when Roman power was in decline.

How different is the look of the soldier emperor Philip the Arabian, recorded in rough marble deliberately left unfinished. With time the Roman portraitists managed to penetrate ever deeper into the human personality. The difficult capricious nature of an ageing woman, bitterness and fatigue can be read in the portrait of Julia Cornelia Salonina, the wife of Emperor Gallienus. A grimace of suffering, doubt and fear distorts the face of Balbinus, an unwilling emperor who was killed by his own guards. The gem of the collection is an exquisite, animated female portrait from the 160s, known as The Syrian Woman. With almost invisible transitions, the smooth modelling of volumes brings out in the marble the fine, tender face of a woman with eastern features and a captivating highly subtle play of melancholy emotions and thoughts.

As well as sculpture in the round, the Hermitage also possesses Roman reliefs. Superb examples can be seen on the sides of marble sarcophagi. One depicts a wedding ceremony, another an episode from Euripedes' tragedy Hippolytos. By tradition such scenes reflected the fate of the occupant of the sarcophagus. The ideally handsome bodies of youths and maidens and narrative details linked by a measured rhythm convey the idea of the beauty of the human being and earthly life, of its triumph over death. This idea also inspired decorative sculpture, which is on display in the next two halls.

< Bust of Empress Salonina
Mid-3rd century A.D. Marble
Height: 57 cm (Hall 107)

Sarcophagus
2nd–3rd century A.D. Marble
Height: 116 cm (Hall 107)

Theseus' son Hippolytos, the hero of Euripedes' tragedy, is depicted on the front of the sarcophagus in the scenes that preceded his death: going off hunting and receiving a message from his stepmother Phaedra, who slanders him for rejecting her passionate advances.

Portrait of an Unknown (Syrian) Woman 2nd century A.D. Marble
Height: 30 cm (Hall 107)

The Roman Atrium
Fountain statue: Cupid Riding a
Dolphin. 1st century
Roman copy of a Greek original
Marble. Height: 87 cm (Hall 108)

The Roman Atrium
The Display of Ancient Decorative
Sculpture of the 1st and 2nd
Centuries (Hall 107)

The Roman Atrium
Detail of the interior (Hall 107)

The next hall reproduces the atrium – inner courtyard – of a rich Hellenistic or Roman house. The walls enclose a square area with a floor covered by a stone mosaic. The central part is framed by a colonnade (peristyle). In a proper Roman courtyard, admittedly, the columns did not support anything: they were free-standing, casting a shadow in the hot Italian noon. A fountain always played in the centre of the courtyard; here there is a fountain statue.

The hall displays small-scale decorative sculpture of the first and second centuries – an invariable adornment of the interiors of Roman houses. There are many depictions of children here, a common feature of Roman plastic art in the heyday of the empire, when public and civic ideals gradually began to replace an interest in a person's private life. The statues and peristyle courtyard create a visual impression of unity, a synthesis of architecture and sculpture.

In designing the exhibition halls, Klenze coped superbly with the task of creating an architectural setting corresponding to the character of the works of art on display, aiding their appreciation.

In the large hall beyond the Roman courtyard, statues of gods, goddesses and heroes of ancient mythology are freely spaced by the walls and pillars that are faced with red artificial marble. Lit by a soft diffused light from the high windows, they seem wrapped in air and it is not hard to imagine this decorative monumental sculpture of the Roman-Hellenistic period outdoors, in squares or gardens.

This hall contains one of the Hermitage's most famous ancient statues – the *Taurida Venus*. Exquisite and slender, with lithe elongated forms, a high waist and a small head, the goddess of love and beauty seems the embodiment of grace, daintiness and femininity – the ideal of female beauty in the Hellenistic era, when the traditions of Greek art spread throughout the Ancient World. This second-century Roman work derives from the celebrated Aphrodite of Cnidus, created by Praxiteles, the Greek sculptor of the fourth century B.C. The statue was found in the outskirts of Rome in 1719 and bought on the instructions of Peter the Great, but only in 1721, after long negotiations, did the papal authorities allow its exportation from Italy. In St Petersburg it stood a long time in the Summer Garden, before being moved to the Taurida Palace in the late 1820s. In 1850 Nicholas I ordered that the *Taurida Venus* be moved to the New Hermitage. Chronologically the Hellenistic works in the Taurida Venus Hall continue the display of Ancient Greece on the other side of the New Hermitage vestibule.

The Dionysus Hall*
The Display of Hellenistic Sculpture (Hall 109)

The Taurida Venus
3rd century B.C.
Roman copy of a Greek original
Marble. Height: 165 cm (Hall 109)

The Main Staircase
and the Vestibule of
the New Hermitage

Two-faced kantharos
490–480 B.C.
Craftsman of the
"London group", Attica
Earthenware,
red-figure painting
Height: 17.7 cm (Hall 111)

Portico of the New Hermitage
with statues of Atlantes. 1840s
Architect: Leo von Klenze, with Vasily
Stasov and Nikolai Yefimov;
Sculptor: Alexander Terebenev

Amphora. Circa 540s B.C.
Made by Amazis, Attica
Earthenware, black-figure painting
Height: 31 cm (Hall 111)

The vestibule from Millionnaya Street was the
entrance to the Imperial Hermitage before the
revolution. Its doors first opened to visitors on
5 February 1852. Through the windows you can see
the portico with atlantes (pillars in human form)
created in the studio of the St Petersburg sculptor
Alexander Terebenev to drawings by Klenze. The
titans of Greek mythology, holding the sky on their
shoulders, perform constant service at the entrance
to the museum, the temple of the muses. The main
staircase, like an Ancient Greek *dromos* (the entrance to a sanctuary), leads upwards to the majestic granite columns and doors that open into the
Picture Gallery: the stairs link two worlds: the world
of Western European art above and the Ancient
World below.

The halls of Ancient Greek art present its history
from the earliest works of the Archaic period (sev-

enth-sixth centuries B.C.) to the masterpieces of the Classical (fifth and fourth centuries B.C.) and Hellenistic (third to first centuries B.C.) periods. Here you can see different types and forms of artistic creation. Greek sculpture is represented mainly by Roman copies that echo the great names: Myron, Phidias, Polyclitus and Praxiteles.

Especially valuable is the very rich collection of Ancient Greek pottery, above all Attic vases. Attica was the region of Greece around Athens, the centre of Classical culture and art. Athenian potters occupied a whole quarter of the city – Kerameikos. The display in the hall of Greek ceramics presents all the variety of shapes and techniques. The shape of the vessels was determined by their purpose. A slender narrow-necked *lekythos* would generally have held some aromatic fragrance. But the rare *lekythoi* with a white ground, a precious example of which is the vase with a depiction of the goddess Artemis feeding a swan, were usually ritual funerary vessels. Among the ceramic masterpieces is a *psykter* (a sort of wine-cooler) of *Feasting Hetaerae* signed by the famous vase-painter Euphronius. The painter completed the work of the potter. He used a sharpened stick to trace the outline of a design, filling it with black lacquer in early vessels or leaving it the coloured of fired clay on the red-figure vases of the Classical period. The red-figure image on a background of shining black possessed volume, naturalness and lively expressiveness.

One of the first vase-painters to go over to the red-figure technique created the Hermitage's famous

The Heracles Hall Sculpture:
Cupid Drawing His Bow
Roman copy from the original created by Lysippus in the second half of the 4th century B.C
Height: 133,2 cm (Hall 111)

The Master of Pan. Athens
Lekythos: Artemis and the Swan
5th century B.C.
Painted earthenware Height 38 cm
(Hall 111)

Euphronius (fl. 510–470 B.C.)
Psykter: Hetaerae Feasting
505–500 B.C.
Painted earthenware. Height: 34 cm
Attica, Greece (Hall 111)

Red-figure pelike: The First
Swallow
Circa 510 B.C. Attica
Painted earthenware. Height 37.5 cm
(Hall 111)

Lekythos in the shape
of a sphinx. 5th century B.C.
Attica
Painted earthenware,
gilded Height: 21.5 cm
(Hall 118)

Figured vessel: Siren
4th century B.C. Athens,
Phanagoria
Painted earthenware
(Hall118)

pelike "The Arrival of the First Swallow". The finely-drawn concise composition, masterfully placed on the convex body of the vase unites in a common impulse figures embodying the three ages of Man. An inscription in purple adds sound to their gestures and movements: "Look, a swallow," exclaims the youth. "Indeed, by Hercules," the man replies. "Here it is, spring already," the boy rejoices.

A separate section of the display contains works from the ancient cities founded on the northern Black Sea by Greek seafarers in the sixth and fifth centuries B.C. From the 1830s onwards archaeological investigations in the Crimea and northern Caucasus became one of the main sources for the enlargement of the Hermitage's ancient collections. Sculpture, pottery and the unique and world-famous collection of Ancient Greek gold in the Treasury Gallery create a picture of a vivid original art that absorbed the traditions of the local peoples, but preserved the link with the metropolis. Graves at Phanagoria (on the Taman peninsula, next to the Crimea) yielded up two figured *lekythoi* for aromatic oils that combined pottery with sculpture – an alluring Siren and a beautiful, treacherous Sphinx.

The hall of Cimmerian Bosporus, a Greek state situated on the Kerch Strait, ends the display of the Northern Black Sea. Today this hall contains two exceptionally valuable collections of the Ancient Department: enchantingly exquisite and warm female terracotta statuettes from Tanagra in Greece and the celebrated glyptic collection –carved gemstones with relief (cameos) and incised (intaglios)

The Hall of Hellenism
The Display of Art of
the Northern Black Sea
Coast (Hall 121)

Cameo: Ptolemy II and
Arsinoë II (The Gonzaga
Cameo). Alexandria
3rd century B.C.
Sardonyx 15.7 x 11.8 cm
(Hall 121)

Female statuette. Tanagra
(3rd–1st century B.C.).
Painted terracotta Height 18.5 cm
(Hall 121)

Aphrodite and Eros
Late 4th century B.C. Tanagra,
Greece
Painted terracotta. Height: 18.5cm
(Hall 121)

designs. The Gonzaga Cameo, one of the world's
most famous ancient cameos, bears the family
name of the Dukes of Mantua to whom it once belonged. It is a double portrait of the Egyptian ruler
Ptolemy II Philadelphus and his consort, Queen
Arsinoe, carved from a three-layer sardonyx with
superb use of the shape and colour of the semiprecious stone.

Our brief acquaintance with the Department of
the Ancient World is over. Moving ahead, through
a gallery of Roman statues, we come back to the
Kolyvan Vase. But do not rush to leave the distant
past. Go by the vase, turn right and follow the pas-
sage to the Winter Palace to reach the hall of Ancient Egyptian art.

The Winter Palace

The Hall of Ancient Egyptian
Culture and Art (5th millennium
B.C. to 1st millennium A.D.)
(Hall 100)

Statue of the goddess
Mut -Sekhmet
15th century B.C.
Granite. Height: 200 cm
(Hall 100)

Heavy granite and painted wood sarcophagi, stone statues, steles and plaques covered with reliefs, statuettes of people, animals, birds and mysterious animal-like gods, pottery and wooden vessels, in a separate case the mummy of a priest (an exhibit that always stirs the imagination of children and adults) – this is the collection of the culture and art of Ancient Egypt.

Although quite small, it nonetheless reflects fairly well its long history from the fourth millennium B.C. to the sixth century A.D. There are few works from the early pre-dynastic period, the Old and Middle Kingdoms, but they reveal the mysterious beauty of Ancient Egyptian art. The art of the sculptural relief that tells of the "travels" of the soul in the Kingdom of the Dead appears in fragments, outstanding among which is a relief from the tomb of the Old Kingdom high official Nimaatra. The statue of Pharaoh Amenemhat III (nineteenth century B.C.) is a masterpiece of portrait sculpture from the Middle Kingdom. The portrait was an important element in the cult of the dead. A receptacle for the soul, it was supposed to represent the deceased in the Afterlife, to convey his essence. The figure sitting stiffly on the throne wearing a headdress with the sacred asp (*uraeus*) is the embodiment of the divine pharaoh, but with the unique face of a man, who has his place and his names, written on the throne. The ancient traditions were developed in the art of the New Kingdom, which is richly represented in the Hermitage. A vivid example of the monumental religious sculpture of this era is a statue of the Mut-Sekhmet from the temple complex of Luxor. The goddess of war and baking heat is depicted as an enthroned

woman with a lioness's head, holding the ankh – a symbol of life. Her figure, formed from large surfaces and near right-angles, seems inseparable from the granite monolith from which the sculptor's hand "extracted" her, softening and animating the stone with skilful polishing and the smoothing of the internal contours. The terrible goddess has a soft femininity about her – she is dangerous when angered, but can be entreated. A superb example of sculptural relief is a stele from the early fourteenth century B.C. depicting the royal scribe Ipi before Anubis, the god of the Underworld. Notable among the portraits from the New Kingdom is the only family group in the Hermitage – Amenemheb, the governor of Thebes, his wife and mother (fourteenth century B.C.). In the display cases are exquisite wooden statues in the traditional conventional style, expressive yet impenetrable. An example of late Egyptian art is a magnificent statue of a queen – Arsinoe or, some researchers believe, the legendary Cleopatra. It displays the influence of the art of the Greeks, who conquered Egypt in 332 B.C. After viewing the display of Ancient Egypt, we return to the New Hermitage and the Council Staircase, by which we ascend to the display of Western European art.

Stele of the royal scribe Ipi
Early 14th century B.C.
Limestone. 95 x 71 cm (Hall 100)

Statuette of a man
Late 15th century B.C.
Wood. Height: 34.5 cm (Hall 100)

Statue of Queen Cleopatra VII
51–30 B.C.
Basalt. Height: 104.7 cm (Hall 100)

The Old Hermitage

The Old Hermitage. 1771–87
Architect: Yury Velten

The Hall of Italian Primitives
Room of Italian Art of the 13th
and 14th Centuries
Architect: Andrei Stakenschneider
(Hall 207)

The Council Staircase
The upper landing

The Council Staircase begins at the entrance that in the nineteenth century served the premises of the State Council on the ground floor of the Old Hermitage (as the building put up by Yury Velten in 1771–87 along the Neva next to the Northern Pavilion of the Small Hermitage became known after the opening of the New Hermitage). In the first hall we enter Catherine II played billiards and kept her paintings. In the 1850s this hall and those that follow were redecorated by Andrei Stakenschneider for Alexander II's eldest son. Now they house a display of Italian Renaissance art (1200s–1500s).

The first hall contains the "Primitives" – the earliest paintings. In essence these are still mediaeval works – icons with a stylized golden background and immobile, almost incorporeal figures of saints in colourful clothing, with austere spiritual faces. But even one of the greatest masters of the Late Gothic, the Sienese painter Simone Martini, invests the Virgin in his *Annunciation* (half of diptych, a two-part composition – the other panel with the Archangel Gabriel is in Washington D.C.) with the grace and elegance of a noble lady and it seems the Psalter she holds is a secular book. There is a legend that Laura, the ideal beloved extolled by the artist's friend, the famous scholar and poet Petrarch, served as a model. The first observations of reality in fourteenth-century painting were a reflection of the emerging Humanist world view, the inception of more realistic art.

Even without works by the founding-father of this new direction, Giotto (1266–1337), the Primitives in the Hermitage provide an idea of the Proto-Renaissance innovations that prepared for the blossoming of the Quattrocento – the Early Renaissance of the

1400s. Its main centre was Florence. The four halls along the Neva that follow are devoted to fifteenth-century Florentine painting. They vividly demonstrate the discovery of the beauty in the earthly world and human beings, and bold artistic experiments. A piece of frescoed wall (a rare exhibit for a museum) demonstrates a striving to depict three dimensions. Although the standing figures of St Dominic and Thomas Aquinas are the same height as the seated Virgin, as in mediaeval works, the folds of their clothing indicate the rounded volume of their bodies and their faces display individual character: it is believed that fellow monks posed for Fra (Brother) Beato Angelico, one of the most poetic artists of the Quattrocento. In his *Madonna with Angels* the divine and earthly combine in a sublime image of tenderness and purity. In search of means to depict the real world, the artists of the 1400s drew on ancient art. The sculptor Giovanni della Robbia employed a classical architectural order to decorate an altar, but he embellished the Ionic columns and frieze with garlands of fruit and filled his *Nativity* with vivid details from Italian rural life.

A fondness for lively detail and a narrative element are characteristic features of Quattrocento art. The painting by Bernardino Fungai on a panel from a cassone chest colourfully "tells a tale": the Ancient Roman general Scipio Africanus surrounded by figures

Fra Beato Angelico da Fiesole
(Circa 1400–1455)
Madonna and Child with Angels.
Circa 1425
Tempera on panel 80 x 51 cm
(Hall 209)

Fra Beato Angelico da Fiesole
(Circa 1400–1455)
Madonna and Child with
St Domenic and St Thomas
Aquinas
Circa 1424–30. Fresco. 196 x 187 cm
(Hall 209)

Giovanni della Robbia
The Nativity. Early 16th century
Majolica. 262 x 167 cm
(Hall 209)

< Simone Martini (1284 – ca1344)
The Virgin from an Annunciation
Circa 1340–44
Tempera on panel. 30.5 x 21.5 cm
(Hall 207)

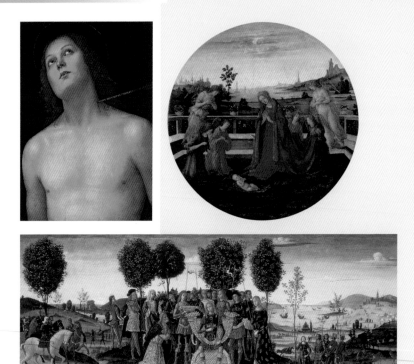

Perugino (Pietro Vannucci)
(1450–1523). Saint Sebastian
Circa 1495
Oil on panel 53.5 x 39.5 cm (Hall 213)

It was not the suffering
of the early Christian martyr,
riddled with arrows, that attracted Perugino in the image
of St Sebastian, but the beauty
of the young body, rediscovered by Early Renaissance artists. This is one of the earliest
depictions of a nude model
in Italian art.

Filippino Lippi (Circa 1457–1504)
The Adoration of the Christ-Child
Mid-1480s
Oil on copper, transferred from panel
Diameter 53 cm (Hall 213)

Bernardino Fungai (1460–1516)
The Magnanimity of Scipio
Africanus
Oil on panel. 62 x 166 cm (Hall 212)

in modern dress, horsemen, warriors and a finely
drawn Tuscan landscape.

In the Early Renaissance, landscape supplanted
the gold backgrounds of the Primitives. This was
aided by the study of the laws of perspective.
The valleys, hills and mountains receding into the
distance in the exquisite tondo (round painting)
of the *Adoration*, delicate spires above the horizon
and a soft golden light from the heavens create an
atmosphere of quiet mystery for the sacred scene.
This is a work by Filippino Lippi, the son of the
famous Filippo Lippi. He was a talented representa-
tive of the last generation of Quattrocento artists,
as was Perugino (Pietro Vannucci), whose paintings
complete the Early Renaissance section. His St Sebastian and Portrait of a Young Man anticipate the
images of the ideal harmonious personality produced by the artists of the following era, the High
Renaissance.

Heavy doors decorated with brass, tortoiseshell
and gilded bronze open into the main hall of the
Old Hermitage. Columns of grey marble, porphyry
and jasper, white marble fireplaces, reliefs, decora-

tive painting – all this sumptuous imitation-Baroque interior serves as a setting for a pair of the Hermitage's treasures: two of the no more than fourteen surviving paintings by the great Leonardo da Vinci.

The *Benois Madonna*, an early work, is a step away from the Quattrocento towards a more profound grasp of the world. Having established the connection between light and three-dimensional forms, Leonardo models them with subtle gradations of light and shade (*sfumato*), placing the figures in the natural setting of a shady room. It is linked to the wider world by the light from the window; its centre is the Mother and Child. They are united by a common sense of discovery, a first perception of the world, reflected in the serious look of the Child, and the joy of motherhood lighting up the face of the young Mary.

The *Litta Madonna* is a mature work. In it the great artist ascends to the peaks of understanding the beauty of the world and the human being, pursuing complete harmony of material and spiritual elements. The appearance of the Virgin in this moment of intimate contact with her Son, her face touched by shadows and fleeting smile convey profound emotion, enlivening her classic beauty with the tender light of maternal love. The harmonious

Leonardo da Vinci (1452–1519)
Madonna with a Flower
(The Benois Madonna). 1478
Oil on canvas, transferred from panel
49.5 x 33 cm (Hall 214)

The Leonardo da Vinci Hall
1858–60. Architect:
Andrei Stakenschneider (Hall 214)

Leonardo da Vinci (1452–1519)
The Litta Madonna. Circa 1490–91
Oil on canvas, transferred from panel
42 x 33 cm (Hall 214)

The paintings by Leonardo da Vinci are named after their owners before the Hermitage. The *Madonna with a Flower* was bought in 1914 from the Benois collection in Petrograd; the second work was bought in 1865 from Count Litta in Milan.

Francesco Melzi (1493–1570)
Female Portrait, Flora. Circa 1520
Oil on canvas. 76 x 63 cm (Hall 215)

Correggio (Antonio Allegri)
(1489/94–1534)
Female Portrait. Circa 1519
Oil on canvas. 103 x 87.5 cm (Hall 215)

Jacopo da Pontormo (Jacopo
Carucci) (1494–1557)
Madonna and Child with Saint
Joseph and John the Baptist
1521–22
Oil on canvas 120 x 98.5 cm (Hall 216)

> Domenico Cadriola
(1494–1528)
Portrait of a Man (?). 1512
Oil on canvas. 117 x 85 cm

ideal of beauty was the chief attainment of High
Renaissance art (late fifteenth – first quarter of the
sixteenth century), which is very well represented
in the Hermitage.

Beyond the Da Vinci hall is a splendid female
portrait by his pupil, Francesco Melzi. The classi-
cally ideal image, in the spirit of Leonardo, suggests
that this may be the goddess Flora. A different female image, full of dignity and subtle intellect, oc-
curs in a rare portrait by the celebrated Parmesan
painter Correggio: mourning dress, laurels – a symbol of poetic gifts, and ivy – signifying eternal love,
a cup with a draught of sorrow and oblivion, to
judge by the probably Homeric quotation on it,
point to the woman's widowhood.

The last hall of the Old Hermitage presents
Mannerism (last three quarters of the sixteenth
century) reflecting the crisis of the Late Renaissance. The rejection of the principles of harmony
and a search for a personal, subjective "manner"
found expression in the arbitrary proportions,
chromatic and rhythmic dissonances of the agitated, tragically anguished paintings by Jacopo Pontormo and Giovanni Battista Rosso and in the
abstracted decorativeness and cold eroticism of
Giulio Romano.

From the hall of Mannerism, we walk back on
the other side of the Old Hermitage, to view the
Venetian Renaissance art.

The first hall of the display is closest to the
Primitives and contains works of the early Venetian Renaissance that began later than in Florence,

46

only in the mid-1400s. The long ties between Venice and Byzantium with its rich colouristic traditions in art and the very air of the "Queen of the Adriatic" engendered a passion for colour. Colour became the main means of expression for the Venetian school. Venetian art developed with rapid brilliance.

By the end of the fifteenth century Venice produced the first great master of the High Renaissance – Giorgione. A plague epidemic cut short his life at the age of 32 and he left less than a dozen paintings. One of the most celebrated is the Hermitage's *Judith*, depicting the apocryphal heroine who saved her people by seducing and then beheading the enemy general Holofernes. Lit by the first rays of the sun that flare up in cold fire on her clothing, she is calm and beautiful like an ancient goddess as she tramples on the head of her defeated foe, whose face bears the frozen grimace of death and smile of bliss.

The harmonious ideal of the human personality acquired in the Venetian language of colour sensual fullness and psychological expressiveness. An intense spiritual life heightens the proud dignity and nobility in the Venetian portrait, which is represented in the display by the works of Domenico Caprioli, Jacopo Palma the Elder and Lorenzo Lotto.

Giorgione (Giorgio da Castelfranco) (Circa 1478–1510). Judith
Oil on canvas, transferred from panel
144 x 66.5 cm (Hall 217)

Palma the Elder
(Jacopo Negretti) (1480–1528)
Portrait of a Young Man. 1510s
Oil on canvas. 93.5 x 72 cm (Hall 218)

Titian (Tiziano Vecellio)
(1488/90–1576)
Saint Sebastian. 1570s
Oil on canvas. 210 x 115.5 cm (Hall 221)

Titian (Tiziano Vecellio)
(1488/90–1576). Danaë
Between 1546 and 1553
Oil on canvas 120 x 187 cm
(Hall 221)

Titian (Tiziano Vecellio)
(1488/90–1576)
The Repentant Mary Magadalene
1560s
Oil on canvas. 119 x 97 cm
(Hall 221)

Titian (Tiziano Vecellio)
1488/90–1576
Christ the Pantocrator. Ca 1570
Oil on canvas. 96 x 80 cm
(Hall 221)

> Veronese (Paolo Caliari)
(1528–1588)
The Lamentation
Between 1576 and 1582
Oil on canvas. 147 x 111.5 cm
(Hall 222)

The works of Titian occupy a central place in the Venetian Renaissance display. The nine works by the great painter in the Hermitage span almost his entire career. The painter's genius and the power of his palette manifested themselves fully in the 1540s and 1550s. *Danae* is one of four paintings that Titian did on the mythological subject of the daughter of King Acrisius, locked up to keep her chaste, who became a mistress of Zeus. The beauty of her naked body is warmed by life, passion and the joy of earthly love. The same Venetian Renaissance ideal is embodied in *The Repentant Mary Magdalene*. Gold in a host of shades colours both the figure and the landscape that uneasily echoes her passionate emotion, animating the beautiful human flesh. But harmony between human being and the world gives way to conflict in Titian's last works, painted as Renaissance ideals collapsed. Tragic chaos surrounds his *St Sebastian*. Yet Titian's faith in humanity remains strong: Sebastian, like an ancient hero, beautiful and strong of spirit challenges the world and keeps his dignity.

On display in the next hall are works by members of Titian's school. *The Lamentation*, painted by Paolo Veronese, one of Titian's most gifted pupils, for the Church of San Giovanni i Paolo in Venice, is striking for its monumental composition and powerful colour scheme. The burning tone of the figure of the young John, full of life and passion, contrasts with the greenish hues of the dead, yet powerful and beautiful body of Christ. These are Life and Death in noble aspect linked by the love of the Virgin.

The Venetian display ends with works of applied art – fabrics, glass and artistic bronze, everything for which the Adriatic republic was famous. Venetian glass was noted for its exquisite forms and workmanship. The industry began in the thirteenth century and was soon centred on the island of Murano in the lagoon. It reached its peak in the Renaissance era. One of the Venetian glassmakers' most refined techniques was *latticino*, in which threads of white or other opaque glass were incorporated into the body of a vessel to form a fine filigree pattern.

We pass back though the hall of Mannerism to reach the Hermitage Theatre.

Jug, bowl and reliquary
of St Barbara
Late 15th – early 16th century
Venice
Blue, pink and clear glass, painted
with coloured enamels, gilding
(Hall 223)

Venetian fabric. Detail
(Hall 223)

Jug of blue glass
Late 16th – early 17th century
Venice (Hall 223)

The Hermitage Theatre

View of the Hermitage Theatre
from the Neva

The Hermitage Theatre
The auditorium and stage. 1783–85
Architect: Giacomo Quarenghi

The Foyer of the Hermitage
Theatre. 1783, 1902
Architects: Yury Velten; Leonty Benois
(Hall 225)

> The Raphael Loggias (1783–92)
Architect Giacomo Quarenghi
(1744–1817). Copy of Raphael's
frescoes in the Vatican Palace
(Hall 227)

Visible through the windows of the last hall in the Old Hermitage is the Hermitage Theatre. The majestic High Classical building with gigantic snow-white columns was constructed by the great architect Giacomo Quarenghi (1744–1817), completing the ensemble of Catherine II's Hermitage. The Italian created the round auditorium within the old Winter Palace of Peter the Great, preserving its internal walls and foundations. Some two centuries later, during a restoration in the 1980s, this made it possible to recreate the personal rooms of Peter I.

The theatre is linked to the Hermitage buildings by a covered walkway on an arch spanning the Winter Canal that was built by the architect Yury Velten.

The entrance to it is immediately beyond the Hall of Mannerism. The light-filled gallery, with the Neva and the canal beyond its high windows, serves as the foyer of the theatre. It was decorated in the French Rococo style by the architect Leonty Benois in 1902. The doors to the theatre are only opened for performances. Inside six semicircular tiers of benches, like in an ancient amphitheatre, descend from the rear wall with elegant columns and statues of Apollo and the muses in niches, to the stalls in front of the stage.

The New Hermitage

Leaving the foyer and continuing on our route, we arrive at an elegant gallery. Thirteen arches run away into the distance; between them are mirrors and tall windows through which light pours, flickering on walls that are covered with exquisite colourful ornament. Arabesques, garlands, masks, figures of people, birds and animals, mythological scenes and landscapes subordinated to the strict logic of the architecture create an air of beauty, joy and harmony. The great Italian Renaissance artist Raphael designed this grotesque ornament inspired by murals in the *grotte* – the remains of Nero's Golden House in Rome, rediscovered in the early 1500s. The gallery is a unique reconstruction of the famous loggias in the Vatican that were built by Bramante in 1517–19 and decorated by Raphael and his pupils. At Catherine II's request, Quarenghi reproduced the loggias in a building running along the Winter Canal. Attached to its walls and vaults are copies of Raphael's frescoes made on canvas by a group of artists led by Christoph Unterberger. The grotesques frame pictures on scriptural subjects known as "Raphael's Bible". Despite certain changes in the details of the arrangement and the dry manner in which the copies were made, the Hermitage gallery does give an idea of the remarkable sixteenth-century ensemble.

When the New Hermitage was constructed, the Raphael Loggias were incorporated into the new building. The adjoining hall was decorated in a similar style.

The Raphael Loggias
Detail of the ceiling painting
From the original by the architect
Donato Bramante
(Hall 227)

The Raphael Loggias (1783–92)
Detail of the wall painting
(Hall 227)

Plate: The Fall of Phaeton. 1522
By G. Andreoli. Gubbio
Majolica, painting over white opaque
tin glaze, lustre. Diameter 25.5 cm
(Hall 229)

The Raphael Hall (Hall of
16th-Century Italian Majolica)
Architect: Leo von Klenze (Hall 229)

Dish depicting St Cecilia
Between 1540 and 1545
Deruta. Majolica, painting over white
opaque tin glaze, lustre
Diameter 41 cm

Majolica Vessel
Early 16th century. Italy
Painted tin-glazed earthenware
Height: 40 cm

The decoration of this hall, with a portico opening onto the semicircular area at its end, borrows its ornamental motifs from Pompeii and Herculaneum: dancing muses, griffons and stars on the walls; golden electrotype figures of genii and caryatids beneath the coffered ceiling.

The Renaissance-style architecture became a natural setting for the works of Italian Renaissance art that replaced the display of cameos here in the twentieth century. Among them are works by Raphael's pupils: a fountain sculpture of *A Dead Boy and a Dolphin* attributed to Lorenzo Lorenzetti, a cartoon by Giulio Romano for a tapestry in a series on the life of the Ancient Roman general Scipio Africanus. The sixteenth-century tapestry of *Apollo* and the *Signs of the Zodiac* on the wall and carved walnut furniture – *cassoni*-chests for clothing and dowries, a *casa-panca* and the chair of a banker-money-changer – present the applied art of Renaissance Italy.

Particularly well represented here is the famous Italian majolica – monumental dishes, bowls and plates, including wedding pieces and apothecaries vessels. Majolica is a type of ceramic that came to Italy by way of the island of Majorca, from where it got its name: earthenware was covered with an opaque glaze and decorated with paints that retained their rich brightness despite repeated firings thanks to the secrets of the Italian craftsmen. Around 500 items in one of the world's finest collections of Italian majolica demonstrate the skills of ceramists from Faenza, Urbino, Deruta, Gubbio and Castel Durante.

Raphael (Raffaello Santi or
Sanzio) (1483–1520)
The Conestabile Madonna
Circa 1503
Oil on canvas, transferred from panel
17.5 x 18 cm (Hall 229)

The Conestabile Madonna was
painted for Count Alfani di
Diamante, whose descendants
married into the Conestabile
family that kept Raphael's
masterpiece for over two and
a half centuries. In 1870 the
family was obliged to sell "the
pearl of Perugia". It was bought
by Alexander II for his wife,
Empress Maria Alexandrovna,
under whose will the painting
passed to the Hermitage in 1880.

The main thing in this hall, though, is two paintings by the great Raphael. The more famous is the *Conestabile Madonna*, the artist's first commission and earliest masterpiece. It already displays the distinctive character that would make him "the Master of the Madonnas". Inscribed in a perfect circle, the finely drawn graceful figure of the mother with a child in her arms in front of green meadows, a lake and snowy peaks comes across as the embodiment of purity, tenderness and sublime sorrow: Raphael's young, fragile and defencelessly feminine Madonna is a mother giving her child for a great redemptive sacrifice. The precious gilded wood frame around the tondo (round painting) is believed to have been made to Raphael's design and was originally one with the painting. In the 1870s the painting was transferred to canvas "for better preservation".

The same mood of dignified sorrow can be detected in the Hermitage's other Raphael, *The Holy Family*. It was obviously influenced by Leonardo da Vinci, whose work Raphael got to know in Florence after leaving his native Perugia. The harmony of forms and pure colours subordinated to a smooth linear rhythm, the unity between the figures linked by a common feeling and the landscape outside reflects the ideal of beauty in Raphael's time.

Raphael will be mentioned again, when you pass through the portico of the Majolica Hall and turn right to enter a small room overlooking the inner courtyard of the New Hermitage.

Raphael (Raffaello Santi or Sanzio)
(1483–1520)
The Holy Family (Madonna and
Child with the Beardless Joseph)
Circa 1506
Tempera and oil on canvas, transferred
from panel. 72.5 x 56.5 cm (Hall 229)

Raphael's *Holy Family* entered
the Hermitage as part of a collection bought in 1778 from
the heirs of the famous early
eighteenth-century Parisian art-
lover Pierre Crozat. One of the
best European collections of
the day, this was among Catherine II's largest acquisitions: 400
paintings, many of which have
become celebrated masterpieces of the Hermitage's picture gallery.

53

Leo von Klenze (1784–1864)
The Cabinet or Hall of Frescoes
of the School of Raphael
(Hall 230)

This hall is the first of a series of "cabinets" along the courtyard side of the New Hermitage. Conceived as a place for the Empress to relax (Nicholas I regarded the Hermitage as a continuation of his residence), it became a display hall after the acquisition of the frescoes in 1861.

Michelangelo (Michelangelo Buonarroti) (1475–1564)
The Crouching Boy. Early 1530s
Marble. Height: 54 cm (Hall 230)

It is believed that Michelangelo made the *Crouching Boy* for the Medici family sepulchre in the church of San Lorenzo in Florence. In the mid-eighteenth century it was in the collection of the British bank director Lyde-Browne that Catherine II bought in 1785.

On the walls of this hall are nine frescoes (transferred to canvas) on myths about the goddess Venus painted by pupils of Raphael for a villa in Rome. The main exhibit here is the only work in Russia by the great Michelangelo. Walk around this fairly small statue without rushing, look at it from the back and the sides. You can see how the shapes emerge "of themselves" – the muscles of a strong young body in a tense pose: the back arched, the head almost touching the knees. The powerful effort of the body, its resistance to a chance circumstance takes on the character of a dramatic struggle, a clash between human will and Fate. This is the central theme of Michelangelo's art, in which the idea of harmony for the first time gave way to a tragic sense of discord, of conflict between Man and the world. It is no coincidence that Michelangelo had such a strong influence on Late Renaissance artists. Two large paintings from that period complete the display of the Italian Renaissance.

To see them, we need to return to the Majolica Hall and turn immediately right, into a large hall lit from above. Opposite the entrance are two immense canvases by the last great Venetians of the period: *The Conversion of Saul* by Paolo Veronese and *The Birth of John the Baptist*, a masterpiece by Tintoretto. The scale of this multi-figure composition, choppy rhythms and contrasts of colour give it an agitated, almost dramatic character. A dramatic perception of the world would remain a characteristic of art in the new phase of its history, the seventeenth century. This hall presents the

main tendencies in Italian art that arose at the turn of the new century. In the 1580s the Carraccis, two brothers and a cousin, founded the Bologna Academy. This school drew on the study of the classical legacy of the High Renaissance to develop a new style, austere, clear and majestic. A vivid example is a painting by Annibale, the foremost Carracci – *The Holy Women at the Tomb*, a sort of centre around which are grouped works by other prominent representatives of this tendency: Guido Reni, Guercino and Carlo Dolci.

The opposite pole to Academicism was the tendency to realism that appeared in the early 1600s and found its most powerful expression in the art of the brilliant reformer of painting, Caravaggio. *The Lute-Player* – the only Caravaggio in the Hermitage – is an eloquent image of the beauty and transience of youth. This highly-gifted artist challenged the classical norms and ideals. His personages are from the Roman crowd; the "beautiful" for him lies in the material flesh of things; his language is contrasts of light and shade that give drama to a scene – a device known as tenebrism that attracted many painters. The main trend in Italian art in the seventeenth century and beyond was the Baroque. The display devoted to it is in the adjoining hall to which we now move.

Carlo Dolci. 1616–1686
St Cecilia. Circa 1670
Oil on canvas. 126 x 99.5 cm
(Hall 237)

Tintoretto (Jacopo Robusti) (1518–1594). The Nativity of John the Baptist. Circa 1550
Oil on canvas. 181 x 266 cm
(Hall 237)

Annibale Carracci (1560–1609)
The Holy Women at the Tomb
1597–98
Oil on canvas 121 x 145.5 cm
(Hall 237)

Caravaggio (Michelangelo Merisi dei Caravaggio) (1571–1610)
The Lute-Player. Circa 1595
Oil on canvas. 94 x 119 cm
(Hall 234)

The Large Italian Skylight Hall
Archittect Leo von Klenze (Hall 238)

Giuseppe Mazzuola (1644–1725)
The Death of Adonis. 1709
Marble. Height: 193 cm (Hall 238)

Giovanni Battista Tiepolo
(1696–1770)
The Triumph of a General
Circa 1725
Oil on canvas. 546 x 322 cm (Hall 238)

Larger than the previous one and again with a glazed ceiling, this hall is known as the Large Skylight Hall, the two either side as the Small Skylight Halls. Light from above, huge bare windowless walls covered in matte paint imitating cloth – Klenze specifically designed this area for the hanging of large paintings. Yet at the same time he gave the halls palatial splendour. The vaults are embellished with gilded mouldings; in the centre are monumental ornaments of semiprecious stone – lapis-lazuli in the Small Skylight Hall, malachite in the Large.

In the very middle of the room stands a marble statue of Adonis, beloved of the goddess Aphrodite, and the wild boar that according to myth tore him to pieces while he was hunting. The complex S-like arrangement of the figure, the dynamic turn giving a host of different viewing angles, the virtuoso finish on the marble – polished to a shine on the youth's body with fine details that show up in the light in contrast to the carved relief of the tousled hair and the stiff hatching on the dense mass of the beast's body create an image that is dramatic and at the same time strikingly decorative. This characteristic Baroque work is by Giuseppe Mazzuola, a pupil of the great Lorenzo Bernini.

Italian Baroque art is represented in this hall by a variety of names, schools and genres. Venetian painting reached another glorious peak in the 1700s. It is easy to imagine the monumental canvases of the eighteenth-century Venetian painter Giovanni Battista Tiepolo in the sumptuous hall of some palace. He opened up space to the depths and filled it with many figures; his paints are rich

and bright, applied in a broad manner with light used to give accents. This series on subjects from Ancient Roman history, five of which are now in the Hermitage, was indeed created for the Venetian palazzo of Dionisio Dolfino, the Patriarch of Aquileia.

Now, when Venice was less celebrated for its might than for its art – the city's beauty, architecture, painting, theatre and masquerades – a new genre of painting was born there: the *veduta* or urban landscape. Among paintings by outstanding exponents of the *veduta*, such as Francesco Guardi and Michele Marieschi, a special place is occupied by a masterpiece by the genre's chief creator, Canaletto (Antonio Canal). All the richness of painting and all the uniqueness of the city – its palaces, churches, squares and embankments, gondolas rocking on the dark water, a procession of envoys and the colourful Venetian crowd – seem to have arisen on this canvas from the coloured air of Venice drunk with sun and moisture.

More austere in line, but just as rich in colour and energetic form, feelings and action is the Baroque painting of Genoa, Venice's age-old rival on the seas. The Genoese school is primarily represented by the works of one of its greatest seventeenth-century masters – Bernardo Strozzi. The significance of the event and the persuasiveness of the painting, as well as the vivid expression of feelings, set Strozzi's depiction of the pious Tobit being cured of blindness apart from many of his other works.

Canaletto (Antonio Canal) (1697–1768)
The Reception of the French Ambassador in Venice. 1720s
Oil on canvas 181 x 229.5 cm (Hall 238)

Bernardo Strozzi (1581–1644)
The Healing of Tobit. Circa 1635
Oil on canvas. 158 x 223.5 cm
(Hall 238)

Michele Marieschi (1696–1743)
The Rialto Bridge in Venice
Circa 1740
Oil on canvas, transferred from panel
130 x 195.5 cm (Hall 238)

Luca Giordano (1632–1705)
The Battle between the Lapiths
and the Centaurs
Late 17th Century
Oil on canvas. 255 x 390 cm (Hall 238)

According to Greek myth,
a fight broke out at the marriage of the king of the Lapiths
between his tribe and the centaurs – half-men, half-horses,
who tried to carry off the
women present.

Alessandro Magnasco
(Lissandrino) (1667–1749)
The Bandits' Rest. 1710s
Oil on canvas. 112 x 162 cm (Hall 238)

Salvator Rosa (1615–1673)
The Prodigal Son
First half of the 1650s
Oil on canvas. 253 x 201 cm (Hall 238)

Membership of a particular school did not
mean that an Italian artist was tied to a specific
place. The Neapolitan Luca Giordano, creator of
the colourful *Battle between the Lapiths and Centaurs* with its impressive sweep and energy, was
famed for the number of his works and the speed
with which he painted. He worked in many major
Italian centres – Naples, Rome, Florence, and Ber-
gamo, and even Toledo in Spain. Direct contacts
between painters of different schools, influencing
each other, helped to expand and enrich the artistic language of Baroque painting. In his striving to
make painted images closer to reality Giuseppe
Maria Crespi, a member of the Bolognese academ-
ic school who worked in his native Bologna and
in other north Italian cities, moved from Bolog-
nese-style idealization to Baroque expression and
truth-to-life. The contrasts of light and shade that
create an atmosphere of sacramental mystery
in *The Death of St Joseph* bear a perceptible resemblance to the work of the Genoese artist Alessandro Magnasco, whom Crespi knew and rated
highly. The Large Skylight Hall contains characteristic landscapes by Magnasco – early ones with

figures of brigands and tramps among classical ruins (*The Bandits' Rest*) and the more mature *Seashore* and *Mountain Landscape*. Painted in gloomy olive-earthy tones with unexpected bursts of light, they are infused with a sense of the transience of a world immersed in darkness and decay. Magnasco's paintings and the melancholy images, close in mood, of the Neapolitan painter, actor and writer Salvator Rosa form a pre-Romantic tendency in Italian Baroque art. Its other extreme was purely decorative painting, characteristic of which are the vedute of Bernardo Bellotto. That Venetian painter, a nephew and pupil of Canaletto, worked almost all his life outside Italy – in Vienna, Munich, Dresden and Warsaw. The series of views of Dresden and nearby Pirna display Bellotto's almost documentary accuracy in depicting the world. After completing our acquaintance with the Italian collection, we move on to Spanish painting.

Passing through the Spanish Skylight Hall (to which we shall return), we enter the smaller cabinets to the right.

Bernardo Bellotto (1720–1780)
Pirna from the Right Bank of the Elbe. Between 1747 and 1755
Oil on canvas 133.5 x 237.5 cm
(Hall 238)

Alessandro Magnasco (Lissandrino) (1667–1749)
Seashore. 1720s
Oil on canvas. 158 x 211 cm (Hall 238)

Giuseppe Maria Crespi (1665–1747)
The Death of St Joseph
Circa 1712
Oil on canvas. 234 x 187 cm (Hall 238)

Giuseppe Maria Crespi's painting was inspired by apocryphal popular legend, rather than Scripture: Christ miraculously appears at the death-bed of St Joseph, the husband of the Virgin.

The display of Spanish painting of the 1400s to early 1600s
The Spanish Cabinet (Hall 240)

Luis de Morales (between 1520 and 1525–1585)
Virgin and Child with a Distaff in the Form of a Cross
Oil on canvas, transferred from panel. 71.5 x 52 cm (Hall 240)

Juan Pantoja de la Cruz (1553–1608). Portrait of Diego de Villamayor. 1605
Oil on canvas. 89 x 71 cm (Hall 240)

El Greco (Domenikos Theotokopoulos) (1541–1614)
The Apostles Peter and Paul
Between 1587 and 1592
Oil on canvas. 121.5 x 105 cm (Hall 240)

A Greek from the island of Crete, who grew up on the traditions of Byzantine icon-painting and the Italian Renaissance, El Greco became Spain's first great painter. Contrasts of colour, angles of view, poses and gestures vividly reveal both spiritual unity and differences of character – the gentle, thoughtful Peter and the uncompromising Paul.

W e are now in the Spanish Cabinet that contains early works of Spanish painting. The Renaissance arrived late in Spain, only in the sixteenth century. In 1492 the country completed the Reconquista – an 800-year struggle to free the Iberian peninsula from the Moors. The reconquest united the Spanish people around the Crown and the Church, encouraged a deep Christian faith and a sense of national pride.

All this found reflection in austere, highly dramatic Spanish painting. Deep spirituality links the *Depositions* that can be seen here, naively pure and sincere images still mediaeval in essence, with the tragically exalted *Virgins* of Luis de Morales, one of the outstanding artists of the sixteenth century, with the proud grandee in armour with an unhandsome arrogant face painted by the court portraitist Juan Pantoja de la Cruz and with the apostles Peter and Paul in El Greco's masterpiece.

We return now to the Spanish Skylight Hall that contains the bulk of one of the best collections of Spanish painting outside of Spain. It formed in the early nineteenth century on the back of a general wave of interest in that country's art, which became a revelation for Europe during the Napoleonic Wars. In the eighteenth century the Hermitage had just a few Spanish paintings. In 1814 Emperor Alexander I bought the first-rate collection of the Amsterdam banker Coesvelt and other acquisitions followed. The Hermitage is rich above all in works from the seventeenth century, the Golden Age of Spanish painting. It possesses canvases by all four of the major figures of that period. Two paintings were produced by Spain's greatest Old Master, Diego Velazquez. *Luncheon*, an early work in the *bodegon* genre painted in his native Seville, is marked by the austere Spanish realism that in Velazquez's work acquired depth and significance. A sparse colour scheme, light picking out the faces and figures of the old man, youth and boy from the gloom is not simply a little scene of everyday life. The elements of the modest meal on a cloth lit by golden light – fish, pomegranate, bread and wine – are traditional symbols of Christ. They complete the circle of personages, uniting them in an image with great symbolic meaning. The second Velazquez in the Hermitage is a masterpiece of his mature period – a portrait painted in Madrid around 1640 of the artist's patron, the Count-Duke of Olivares, Philip IV's prime minister and favourite, the effective ruler of Spain.

Diego Velazquez (1599–1660)
Breakfast. Circa 1617–18
Oil on canvas. 108.5 x 102 cm
(Hall 239)

The Spanish Skylight Hall
(Hall 239)

Diego Velazquez (1599–1660)
Portrait of the Count-Duke
of Olivares. Circa 1638
Oil on canvas. 67 x 54.5 cm
(Hall 239)

There are no outward signs of the subject's lofty status, but the powerfully moulded face with a high forehead, heavy chin and firm mouth, the superior, detached expression and the intelligent, slightly suspicious penetrating look of the dark eyes convey the strong, masterful personality of an exceptional man with a complex inner world.

Francisco de Zurbaràn
(1598–1664)
St Larence. 1636
Oil on canvas. 292 x 225 cm
(Hall 239)

José de Ribera (1591–1652)
St Sebastian and St Irene. 1628
Oil on canvas. 156 x 188 cm
(Hall 239)

Francesco de Zurbaràn
(1598–1664)
Girlhood of the Virgin
Circa 1660
Oil on canvas. 73.5 x 53.5 cm
(Hall 239)

Six paintings of Christian saints and martyrs represent the work of José Ribera, one of the first masters of the Golden Age. The choice of Sebastian, a favourite Italian saint, as a subject for one of the Hermitage's best paintings by Ribera and the use of tenebrism – strong contrasts of light and shade, turning the martyr's rescue by St Irene into a mysterious night scene, show the painter to have been a follower of Caravaggio who spent almost all his life in Naples. But his inherent realism and deep religious passion remain truly Spanish.

The third great Spaniard, Francisco Zurbaran, produced large altar paintings for the monasteries and churches of Seville, where he lived his whole life. Of the three Zurbarans in the Hermitage two are genuine world-ranking masterpieces. A typical example of his work is the monumental *St Lawrence*. Lawrence, an early deacon of the Roman church and a saint especially venerated in Spain, is depicted holding the instrument of his martyrdom – a gridiron on which he is supposed to have been roasted. Behind his back is an endless space, a lofty sky, the valleys and mountains of Spain. He himself, although dressed in heavy gold-embroidered robes, is presented as a stocky man with the face of a Spanish peasant inspired by faith for the sake of which he is ready to accept death simply and calmly. Spiritual beauty is presented just as simply and persuasively in the intimate image of the Virgin as a pure, tender girl, a dark-eyed, dark-haired little Spaniard. The extreme sparseness of detail is compensated for by the depth and intensity of colour, the gentle strength of the chromatic

Bartolomé Esteban Murillo
(1617–1682)
Rest on the Flight into Egypt
Between 1665 and 1670
Oil on canvas. 136.5 x 179.5 cm
(Hall 240)

chords struck by the fiery-red dress with the green patch of the prayer-cushion and the white cloth over it and the blue-black cloak.

And, finally, thirteen paintings by Bartolomé Esteban Murillo give a vivid picture of the talent and variety of the work of the painter who brilliantly rounded off the Golden Age. As well as Murillo's well-known monumental compositions on scriptural subjects (*Rest on the Flight into Egypt, Isaac Blessing Jacob, Jacob's Ladder* and *The Immaculate Conception*) his genre painting of *A Boy with a Dog* stands out. This artless urchin dressed in picturesque rags exudes a sense of warmth and immediacy. Painted in a light range of colours, this is a masterpiece of the artist's early, "cold" period. The more intimate types of painting – genre scenes and still lifes – were not common in Spanish art generally. That adds especially value to both Antonio Puga's *Knife-Grinder* and an exceptionally beautiful still life by Antonio Pereda: simple everyday objects – cheese, pastries – and luxurious Eastern-style reminders of Islamic times are here arranged in an austere typically "Spanish" logical order.

The seventeenth century was a Golden Age not only for Spain, but also for other European countries where national schools formed and flourished at that time. A leading place among them was taken by the Dutch and Flemish schools. Both are represented in the Hermitage by very rich collections. The next suite of halls, with windows facing the Small Hermitage, contains Dutch art. We move now to the first of them – the Tent-Roofed Hall.

Bartolomé Esteban Murillo
(1617–1682)
Boy with a Dog. 1650s
Oil on canvas. 74 x 60 cm (Hall 239)

Boy with a Dog and its companion piece *Girl with a Basket of Fruit* (now in the Pushkin Museum, Moscow) are the only Spanish paintings that Catherine II bought in the eighteenth century (as part of the Duc de Choiseul's collection in Paris).

Antonio Pereda (1608–1678)
Still Life. 1652
Oil on canvas. 80 x 94 cm
(Hall 239)

17th-century Dutch Art
The Tent-Roofed Hall
(Hall 249)

Willem Claesz Heda
(1594 – between 1680 and 1682)
Breakfast with a Crab. 1648
Oil on canvas. 118 x 118 cm
(Hall 249)

Frans Hals (between 1581
and 1585–1666)
Portrait of a Young Man Holding
a Glove. Circa 1650
Oil on canvas. 80 x 66.5 cm
(Hall 249)

Pieter de Hooch
(1629 – after 1684)
A Woman and Her Maid
Circa 1660
Oil on canvas. 53 x 42 cm
(Hall 249)

> Jan Porcellis
(Circa 1584–1632)
Sea on a Dull Day
Circa 1630
Oil on panel
47.5 x 63.5 cm
(Hall 249)

Arranged on special stands are the small-format paintings for which the Tent-Roofed Hall was created. These works date from the heyday of the small heroic republic that formed as a result of revolt against Spanish rule in the sixteenth century. Building on the earlier traditions of art in the Low Countries, the Dutch school produced art popular with the victorious burghers. Paintings now adorned not churches (Holland was overwhelmingly Protestant), but the modest houses of city-dwellers: hence the size of the works and the description of the artists: "Small Dutch Masters". Paintings were in great demand. They were produced to order and also for sale on the market. The buyers wanted to see their own lives reflected in them: themselves and their fellow citizens, their city and the surrounding countryside. That is how the genres of Dutch painting formed: portrait, landscape, still life and genre scene. These are all represented in the Hermitage's excep-

Jacob van Ruisdael (1628/29–1682)
The Marsh. 1660s
Oil on canvas 72.5 x 99 cm
(Hall 249)

The Marsh is an outstanding masterpiece by Jacob van Ruisdael. The low horizon and lofty sky of the Dutch landscape are here covered by a wall of huge trees rising above the marsh. Above them is gloom and silence. The water is stagnant and overgrown with plants; a broken piece of tree has fallen in and is rotting. Life is slowly dying away. But through the dense foliage the sky shines with golden clouds and the young forest shoots force their way towards the light; a startled bird rises above the cold waters, seeking space and warmth. Life and death merged into one, the mysterious alluring and frightening beauty of nature – the obsessions of an artist who attained special depth in this work.

tionally full collection of around 1,000 canvases, as a rule by great names and great works. The self-important Dutch burgher can be seen in two works by the best Dutch portraitist Frans Hals, who was able to "blow apart" a respectable exterior with vivid character and temperament. The unprepossessing beauty of northern nature is revealed in the landscapes of Jan van Goyen, Jan Porcellis and Jacob van Ruisdael. Profound meaning enlivens everyday objects lovingly painted in the still lifes of Willem Claesz Heda and Pieter Claesz and in Willem Kalf's sumptuous *Dessert*. Hints and metaphors lie concealed in the seemingly straightforward genre scenes by such famous masters as Pieter de Hooch, Jan Steen, Jan van Ostade and Gerard Ter Borch. The poetry of daily life, a sense of the beauty of reality that led to the discovery of aerial perspective and a tonal colour scheme – the ability to recreate the wealth of colours in the visible world while subordinating them to an overall tone, the colour of the natural medium of light and air – that is what unites Dutch painters.

Holland gave the world one of its greatest artists – Rembrandt. Our meeting with him awaits us at the end of the Dutch exhibition.

Gerard Ter Borch (1617–1681)
The Glass of Lemonade. 1660s
Oil on canvas, transferred from panel
67 x 54 cm (Hall 249)

Rembrandt Harmensz van Rijn
(1606–1669). Danaë. 1636–42
Oil on canvas. 185 x 202.5 cm
(Hall 254)

Rembrandt Harmensz van Rijn
(1606–1669)
Flora. 1634
Oil on canvas 125 x 101 cm (Hall 254)

Rembrandt Harmensz van Rijn
(1606–1669)
Portrait of an Old Man in Red
1652–54
Oil on canvas. 108 x 86 cm (Hall 254)

> Rembrandt Harmensz van Rijn
(1606–1669)
David and Uriah. 1663–65
Oil on canvas. 127 x 116 cm
(Hall 254)

The Hermitage can boast one of the world's best collections of Rembrandt's painting – over twenty paintings spanning the whole of his artistic career. The son of a wealthy Leiden miller, at the age of 16 Rembrandt Harmensz van Rijn left the university to which his father had sent him in order to devote himself to painting. After completing his apprenticeship, he opened a studio in Leiden; then in 1631, encouraged by his successes, he moved to Amsterdam, one of the leading centres of Dutch culture and art. Rembrandt's first decade in Amsterdam was a time when his talent and fortunes flourished and he found love and happiness. In 1634 he married Saskia van Uylenburgh. It was his young wife that the artist depicted in the guise of Flora, the goddess of flowers and spring. In this early masterpiece one can still detect a purely Dutch sense of the beauty of the material world conveyed by the brush of this brilliant colourist – the heavy splendour of the flowers, the play of shades in the silk, the sensual tenderness of the plain, yet likeable face. But the light on the face seeks there something more that just the charm of blooming youth. Rembrandt's light that penetrates beyond the outward veils of existence became the main "protagonist" of a great painting with a tragic fate – the celebrated *Danae*, returned to life by restorers after a terrible act of vandalism. Lit by a warm golden light that emerges from behind the thrown-back bed-curtains and slowly pours across the whole canvas, Danae, a woman not especially young with a sensuous body and irregular facial features, appears before us transformed and beautified by the thrill of her emotions – love, expectation and hope. The beauty of the human being's inner, spiritual world was Rembrandt's chief theme; *chiaroscuro*, the modelling of form by

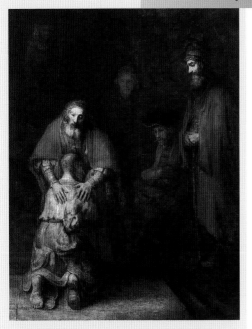

subtle gradations of light and shade, his chief means of expression. With the years, in the works of his mature and late periods, in the 1640s and 1650s, Rembrandt's *chiaroscuro* grew ever more complex and all-embracing; superficial painterly details disappeared from the paintings; they became simpler, more laconic, but the light of spiritual beauty and humanity shone every brighter in them. The light of love, simple motherly concern, warms humble human existence in *The Holy Family*; the fire of the red clothing of the biblical general Uriah and the shadow creeping across his face betray the depth of feeling of a man leaving this life – he is being sent to his death by King David who is infatuated with his wife. On the wavering boundary between light and dark, life and the mysterious gloom of non-existence, the old men in Rembrandt's portraits are an embodiment of the beauty of a wise soul, illuminated by life's trials, by proximity to the truth that reveals itself in old age. A brilliant expression of truth – the simple, but eternal truth of human love is to be found in Rembrandt's last, most famous painting, the summation of his life with all its serious trials, reflections and searchings – the Hermitage's precious treasure, *The Return of the Prodigal Son*.

The seventeenth-century Flemish school is represented in the Hermitage just as fully as Dutch art. To reach the Flemish display we need to return through the Spanish Cabinet and Skylight Hall, then the Gallery of the History of Ancient Painting.

Rembrandt Harmensz van Rijn
(1606–1669)
The Return of the Prodigal Son. 1660s
Oil on canvas. 262 x 205 cm (Hall 254)

A son, who has squandered the inheritance that he received ahead of time, returns as a penniless vagabond to his parents' home – that is the moment in the Gospel parable depicted in Rembrandt's famous painting. A flood of light brightly illuminates the father and son in the foreground and, penetrating into the depths, flares up on the figures of the silent witnesses. The glimmering colour of the son's figure, occasionally bursting into red, "tells" of his wanderings and his coming to his senses perhaps more eloquently than his tattered clothing, worn-out sandals and calloused feet. The face of the aged father glows, his hands warm the body of his son. The warmth and light of fatherly love, understanding, forgiveness and compassion beautify both the human being and the world around him. That is the truth of Rembrandt's art.

Rembrandt Harmensz van Rijn
(1606–1669). The Holy Family. 1645
Oil on canvas. 117 x 91 cm (Hall 254)

The Gallery of the History
of Ancient Painting
Architect Leo von Klenze (1784–1864)
(Hall 241)

Antonio Canova (1757–1822)
The Three Graces. 1813
Marble. Height: 182 cm (Hall 241)

Vase. Mid-19th century
Malachite (Hall 241)

> The display of Western European
arms and armour of the 15th to
17th Centuries. The Knights' Hall
The cavalcade of knights
(Hall 243)

The elegant gallery you have entered runs alongside the Skylight Halls and has an exit to the New Hermitage's Main Staircase. Its walls hold 86 works on subjects of ancient painting that were executed to a programme drawn up by Leo von Klenze, the designer of the building, by the Munich artist Georg Hiltensperger using the Ancient Greek encaustic technique (wax-based paints on copper sheets). The architect, convinced of the educational mission of the museum, intended that the visitor ascending from the halls of antiquity to the gallery of European painting should obtain an idea of its "pre-history", of the European painters' Greek precursors. Relief portraits of famous artists (including Klenze himself) were placed beneath the gallery's nine domes.

In 1862, with the installation of the Campana collection downstairs, recent Western European sculpture was moved to this gallery and the upper landing of the staircase. This is a large and diverse collection, in which a special place is taken by the outstanding early nineteenth-century Roman sculptor Antonio Canova. The gallery contains his famous masterpieces *Cupid and Psyche* and *The Three Graces* (the inseparable goddesses of female beauty and charm) that embody the cold, refinedly sublime ideal of beauty in Neo-Classical art. The exit at the end of the gallery leads to the display of old arms and armour.

Detail of the display
Rondache shield, bourguignotte
helmet, vambrace, gauntlet
Late 1550s
Venice, Italy
Steel inlaid with gold (Зал № 243)

Among the artistic master-pieces in the Knights' Hall are parts of the armour of the Venetian general Ascanio Sforza Pallavicino, ruler of Parma and Piacenza. The helmet, vambrace (arm piece) and round rondache shield of "blued" steel with a reddish tinge are covered with exquisite gold-inlay ornament. In the centre of the shield, on the helmet and couter (elbow piece) is a depiction of a hydra and the owner's Latin motto:
Ut. Cumq. – "Come what may."
Part of a suit of armour
Early 1500s
Nuremberg, Germany
Steel with niello and gilding
(Hall 243)

Tilt armour. 1590
Made by Anton Peffenhauser
Augsburg, Germany
Nielloed and gilded steel
(Hall 243)

This room is known as the Knights' Hall. In the centre by the wall is a cavalcade of mediaeval knights in heavy plate armour. This is a characteristic form of protection known from the fourteenth century onwards. The helmet and visor, body and leg armour consists of between 60 and 160 plates connected by rivets and straps to enable sufficient movement, although a full harness for a knight and his steed could weigh 16–20 kilos. A knight's armour was not only a product of a highly-developed craft, but also a work of art. The display in the Knight's Hall presents the history, different schools of armoury and styles of decoration used in Western Europe between the fifteenth and seventeenth centuries. Both tournament and war equipment made by German, Italian and Spanish craftsmen are on display here: armour, helmets, shields, swords, daggers, halberds and the first examples of firearms – bombards, guns and pistols. They are fascinating for their technical inventiveness and artistic taste. From here we pass through the Twelve-Column Hall to reach the Flemish art.*

* If the Twelve-Column Hall is closed on account of a temporary exhibition, the Flemish display can be reached by way of the Gallery of Ancient Painting and the landing of the Main Staircase.

The Snyders Hall. The display of Flemish art of the 17th and 18th Centuries
(Hall 245)

Jacob Jordaens (1583–1678)
The Bean King. Circa 1638
Oil on canvas. 157 x 211 cm
(Hall 245)

Rural festivities were a typical subject for David Teniers the Younger, an outstanding Flemish genre painter. The Hermitage has over 40 of his paintings.

Frans Snyders (1579–1657)
Fruit Shop
Oil on canvas. 206 x 342 cm
(Hall 245)

David Teniers the Younger (1610–1690)
A Peasant Wedding. 1650
Oil on canvas. 82 x 108 cm
(Hall 245)

Flanders is one of the main regions of modern-day Belgium – the Southern Netherlands that remained under Spanish rule after the revolt of the northern provinces. The spiritual uplift caused by the independence struggle and the economic success of the country laid the foundation for a flourishing of Flemish culture that found its most vivid expression in painting. The Hermitage has over 500 paintings by more than 140 Flemish artists – a collection of world significance. The lower part of the long wall in the room after the Twelve-Column Hall is hung with paintings by Frans Snyders, one of the greatest Flemish masters of the still life. All the abundant bounty of the land and sea is presented in his *Shops*. Fruit and vegetables are crowded together on the tables and the ground; the gifts of the deep are iridescent with all the shades of seawater from emerald green to the subtlest silvery blues. The same sweep and resonant colour are to be found in Pauwel de Vos's hunting scenes. The beauty and richness of the material, sensual world and the affirmation of life are the main themes of Flemish painting. General unrestrained merriment give a sense of the full-

Anthony van Dyck
(1599–1641)
Self-Portrait
Late 1620–1630s
Oil on canvas
116.5 x 93.5 cm
(Hall 247)

ness of life to scene of a popular Flemish winter celebration in Jacob Jordaens best variant of his famous *Bean King*.

All these artists were followers and pupils of the great Rubens. The most outstanding and independent of them was Anthony van Dyck, the best portraitist in Europe. The twenty-four Van Dycks in the next hall reflect all the stages and range of his work. The early *Family Portrait* (possibly the Amsterdam landscapist Jan Wildens and his family) imbued with a sense of tense life; the artist's self-portrait embodying the ideal of the creative personality; the portrait of Virginio Cesarini, animated by thought and passionate conviction; and the depictions of children are all among Van Dyck's finest achievements in the sphere of intimate portraiture. Van Dyck was also a master of and inventor of the formula for the European formal portrait, represented here by images of the English aristocracy in a series of superb works painted in the last years of his life at the court of King Charles I in London.

Anthony van Dyck (1599–1641)
Portrait of Sir Thomas Wharton
Second half of the 1630s
Oil on canvas. 217 x 128.5 cm
(Hall 246)

Anthony van Dyck (1599–1641)
Portrait of Virginio Cesarini (?)
1622–23
Oil on canvas. 104 x 86 cm
(Hall 246)

Anthony van Dyck (1599–1641)
Portrait of Elizabeth and
Philadelphia Wharton
Second half of the 1630s
Oil on canvas. 162 x 130 cm
(Hall 246)

Peter Paul Rubens (1577–1640)
Perseus and Andromeda
Early 1620s
Oil on canvas. 99.5 x 139 cm
(Hall 247)

Perseus and Andromeda,
which entered the Hermitage
in 1769 as part of the collection of the Saxon minister
Count Brühl that Catherine II
bought from Dresden, is
believed to have remained
in Rubens's Antwerp home
right up to his death.

Peter Paul Rubens (1577–1640)
The Union of Earth and Water
Circa 1618
Oil on canvas 222.5 x 180.5 cm
(Hall 247)

The Rubens Hall
The display of Flemish art
of the 17th and 18th Centuries
(Hall 247)

A son of Flanders, heir to the best traditions
of Netherlandish painting, with a profound
grasp of the achievements of Antiquity and
contemporary Italian art, Rubens expressed with
genius the life-affirming spirit of his homeland in
the visual language of the Flemish Baroque that he
created. Rubens's art outgrew national boundaries
and became a phenomenon of universal significance. Over 40 works represent the great artist's
oeuvre in the Hermitage. All its many aspects are
here: monumental compositions on biblical subjects, ancient mythology and history; portraits and
landscapes; sketches and designs for temporary
decorative structures that record the concept and
the living touch of the artist's hand. The gems of
the collection are celebrated masterpieces.

The Descent from the Cross still retains traces
of Rubens's impressions of Italy, but the tense
sense of drama, dynamism and unexpected flares
of burning colour in the figure of the red-headed
Mary Magdalene introduce a Flemish feeling of
life into the classical composition. This turned
into a full-blooded sensuality and a powerful use
of colour in the artist's mature work. Rubens returned from Italy in 1608. From then until his
death he lived in Antwerp, holding the position
of court painter to Isabella of Austria, the regent
of Flanders.

Rubens's profound ties to his homeland and
involvement in its life were quite often directly
reflected in his painting. His response to the wor-
rying problem of the River Scheldt, the mouth
of which was blockaded by the Dutch, was the

famous allegory *The Union of Earth and Water*. But, as always, the artist rose above the specific subject matter to create an image of the triumphant union of the male and female principles in nature, the sources of the eternal renewal and beauty of earthly life.

A victorious hymn to love and life is written in burning colours in *Perseus and Andromeda*, created at a time when Rubens enjoyed fame, love and happiness: the mythical hero Perseus's reward for a brave deed is the love of the princess he has rescued – Andromeda, a red-haired, buxom Flemish woman, an embodiment of femininity and voluptuous beauty.

As well as the monumental canvases that Rubens so loved to paint, our eyes are drawn by the intimate depth, subtle moods and refined colours of the *Portrait of a Lady-in-Waiting to the Infanta Isabella*.

The peak of Rubens's oeuvre is the famous *Bacchus*. The ancient god of wine-making and grape-growing is presented in Rubens's last significant work as the embodiment of the inexhaustible, burdensome power of the corporeal, elemental, material principle of the world, to the affirmation of which the great Fleming dedicated his art.

After viewing the Flemish painting, we leave the New Hermitage and, passing through the next hall and the gallery on the south side of the Hanging Garden, we enter the display of French art in the Winter Palace.

Peter Paul Rubens (1577–1640)
Bacchus. Between 1638 and 1640
Oil on canvas. 191 x 161.3 cm (Hall 247)

Peter Paul Rubens (1577–1640)
Portrait of a Lady-in-Waiting
to the Infanta Isabella. Mid-1620s
Oil on panel. 64 x 48 cm (Hall 247)

Despite its customary title, it has been suggested that *Portrait of a Lady-in-Waiting* is a depiction of Rubens's daughter, who died at the age of twelve; that the brilliant painter's imagination and love enabled him to picture her grown up and blooming.

Peter Paul Rubens (1577–1640)
The Descent from the Cross
Circa 1617–18
Oil on canvas. 297 x 200 cm (Hall 247)

The Adoration of the Magi
Early 16th century
The "High Brow" workshop,
Limoges, France
Painted enamel on copper
Dimensions: 28 x 38.8 cm
(Hall 274)

The Winter Palace

Bowl with the
Montmorency-Laval arms
1510–28
Saint-Porchaire
White clay with brown clay
insets, clear lead glaze
Height: 10. 5 cm;
diameter: 19.5 cm (Hall 273)

Master of the Thuison Altarpiece
The Entry into Jerusalem
Second half of the 15th century
Oil on panel. 116.5 x 51.5 cm (Hall 273)

The Entry into Jerusalem, a panel
from the altarpiece of the ab-
bey at Thuison in Picardy
(northern France), is one of the
earliest French easel paintings.
Low Countries realism combines here with the pure lines
and refinement characteristic
of French taste.

T he rooms on the first floor of the Winter Palace overlooking Palace Square were once the
living apartments of Catherine II and after the
1837 fire guest accommodation. Since the palace
was transferred to the Hermitage in 1926, they
have been museum halls. They are used to display
the collection of fifteenth- to eighteenth-century
French art that is the second richest in the world
after the Louvre.

The display opens with the French Renaissance. The peace that followed the end of the
Hundred Years' War, a new sense of nationhood
and consolidation around the monarchy, as well
as the influence of Renaissance Italy set the scene
for a cultural upsurge. The products of the artistic
crafts, that revived earlier and faster than the
monumental arts, testify to a renewal and reas-
sessment of the old Gothic forms and the birth of
a new kind of art. Allegorical tapestries of the old
mille-fleurs ("thousand flowers") type acquired
personages in the shape of elegant youths dressed
in the manner of the young nobles who in the
early sixteenth century crowded the court of

Francis I, the king with whose reign the French Renaissance truly began.

The enamel industry of Limoges revived with the new painted enamel technique, of which the Hermitage has a remarkable collection. With its similarity to actual painting, the technique furthered more natural images on the portable altars and icons of the period. Then, in the middle of the sixteenth century, as secular culture flourished, a "new school" of monochrome Limoges enamels emerged, decorating not church utensils but elegant tableware with scenes from mythology.

The display also includes precious examples of the famous Saint-Porchaire faience (of which there are no more than 250 in the whole world) – elegant ivory-coloured articles made for aristocratic use and inlaid with coloured clays.

"Rustic ware" pieces represent "the French Leonardo da Vinci", Bernard Palissy, a scholar, engineer and inventor of this new ceramic technique. Dishes covered with a dark blue glaze are decorated with relief likenesses of fish, snakes, plants and seashells, full of the Renaissance sense of intoxication with the beauty of earthly nature.

The new kind of French easel painting is represented by several exhibits, from two early works of the late 1400s, thorough splendid mid-1500s portraits by Corneille de Lyon, Pierre Dumoustier and an unknown artist, to the Lamentation by the Lorraine artist Jacques Bellange, a work marked by the influence of late Mannerism and a mood of anxiety inspired by the tragic civil wars of religion in the late sixteenth century and the crisis of the French Renaissance.

Bernard Palissy (1510–1589)
Dish. Circa 1560
Lead-glazed earthenware 47.5 x 35 cm
(Hall 274)

Corneille de Lyon (Early 16th century – 1575). Female Portrait. Mid-1530s
Oil on panel. 20 x 15.5 cm (Hall 273)

Unknown 16th-Century Artist. Portrait of the Duc d'Anjou(?). Second half of the 16th century
Oil on panel. 48.5 x 32 cm (Hall 273)

Noble restraint, sensitivity and a refined, spiritual mind – that was the ideal combination of personal traits that found expression in the French Renaissance portrait.

Louis Le Main (1600/1610–1648)
The Milkmaid's Family. 1640s
Oil on canvas. 51 x 59 (Hall 276)

A gifted colourist, Le Nain unites the figures and a landscape painted in the subtlest transitions of colour, from thawing cold hues in the depths to warm, rich ones in the foreground with an overall silvery-grey, pearly tone – this is the light and air of the artist's native Picardy in northern France.

Nicolas Poussin (1594–1665)
Tancred and Erminia. 1630–31
Oil on canvas. 98.5 x 146.5 cm
(Hall 279)

The subject of *Tancred* and *Erminia* was taken from Torquato Tasso's epic poem *Jerusalem* Delivered. Erminia cuts of her magical hair in order to use it to heal the knight Tancred who has been wounded in a fight with a giant. Tancred is supported by his friend and squire Vafrin.

The next section is devoted to the 1600s and begins with the works of Simon Vouet and other members of the school he led in the early decades of the century. After the coronation of Henry IV put an end to the French civil wars, the monarchy rallied the nation. Growing absolutism meant royal control over artistic life as well. Vouet, summoned to the court from Rome, and his circle laboured to create a grand decorative style, drawing on the innovations of Italian Classicism and the Flemish Baroque. At the same time, in the provinces far from the court, "Peintres de la Réalité" appeared. The Hermitage has two works from the scanty legacy of one of the foremost "painters of reality", the master of the peasant genre Louis Le Nain. His *Milkmaid's Family* is celebrated for its picturesque quality and for the significance and merit of the images. The striving after order and organization that transformed reality into the

harmonious world of painting is a reflection of French seventeenth-century rationalism – a belief in reason, in the beauty of higher truths and the eternal laws of the universe. This found its most consistent expression in Classicism, the common national style of French art of the "*Grande Siècle*" based upon the Classical principles of Antiquity and the Renaissance. The father of Classicism in painting was Nicolas Poussin. In a separate room allotted to his works we can see famous masterpieces: *Tancred and Erminia*, tinged with the warmth of a "Titianesque" colour scheme and the stir of lofty emotions, a work that affirms the beauty of human self-sacrifice for the sake of good, love and friendship; a highly dramatic *Descent from the Cross*; and *Landscape with Polyphemus*, an image of the all-embracing harmony of nature. Beyond the Poussin hall are works by the great Classical landscape artist Claude Lorrain. The ideal world of nature in his paintings is warmed by the sun, a play of fickle colours and a lyrical atmosphere.

Nicolas Poussin (1594–1665)
Landscape with Polyphemus. 1649
Oil on canvas. 150 x 199 cm
(Hall 279)

Nicolas Poussin (1594–1665)
Late 1620s
The Descent from the Cross
Oil on canvas. 119.5 × 99 cm
(Hall 279)

Claude Gellée, called Lorrain
(1600–1682) Morning
in the Harbour 1640s.
Oil on canvas 74 x 97 cm
(Hall 280)

Nicolas Poussin (1594–1665)
Nymph, Satyr and Putti. 1630s
Oil on canvas. 72 x 56 cm
(Hall 279)

Antoine Watteau
(1684–1721)
An Embarrassing
Proposal. Circa 1716
Oil on canvas. 65 x 84.5 cm
(Hall 284)

Antoine Watteau (1684–1721)
The Capricious Woman. Circa 1718
Oil on canvas. 42 x 34 cm (Hall 284)

Antoine Watteau (1684–1721)
Savoyard with a Marmot
Circa 1716
Oil on canvas. 40.5 x 32.5 cm (Hall 284)

Nicolas Lancret (1690–1743)
The Dancer Camargo. 1730s.
Oil on canvas 44 x 55 cm (Hall 285)

Marie-Anne de Camargo
(1710–1770) was a celebrated
ballerina at the Paris Opera.
One of the most educated
women of her time, she was
friends with the Enlightenment writers Grimm, Helvétius
and Voltaire, who dedicated
his verses to her. This is one of
four variants of her portrait
produced by Lancret in the
style of Watteau's theatrical
compositions.

Beyond the grand Alexander Hall, the large rooms overlooking Palace Square present eighteenth-century France in all its variety – the decline of aristocratic culture, the Age of Enlightenment, the eve of the French Revolution. On the stands by the windows in the second room after the Alexander Hall are the intimate, in contrast to the monumental Classical canvases, masterpieces of Antoine Watteau, the figure from whom eighteenth-century art sprang. His personages are not gods and heroes, but seemingly chance human beings, snatched by the keen eye of the artist from the reality in which he lived his short life: a young Savoyard, found on a deserted small-town square early one morning; a delightful "capricious woman" listening with a pout to the seductive talk of a self-confident suitor; an elegant company in a park melting in a golden haze forming a scene full of vague hints – *a fête galante*, as this genre invented by Watteau came to be known. The exquisitely fine drawing and rich, delicate palette, unknown in Classicism, of these paintings that lay no claim to greatness or lofty ideas give rise to a sense of life and the charm of subtle, indefinable moods. Watteau was the first to express a concept, new for his age, of the beauty of intimate human feelings. Watteau had only two immediate pupils (and those not for long) – Jean-Baptiste Pater and Nicolas

The Hall of Falconet and French 18th-Century Art (Hall 285)

Between 1766 and 1778 Etienne Maurice Falconet worked in St Petersburg, creating his most famous work – the Bronze Horseman monument to Peter the Great. He brought works to Russia and produced more here that are now in the Hermitage: Threatening Cupid (1766–67), Winter (1771) and others.

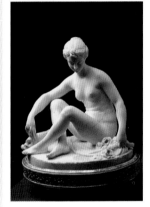

Lancret, whose paintings can be found next-door – but Watteau's genre, subjects and methods that so precisely reflected the tastes and hedonistic spirit of aristocratic society freed from the dictates of absolutism found development in the decorative Rococo (a name related to the word *rocaille* used for its typical ornamental rock-and-shell work), the dominant style of French art in the 1730s–50s. The central hall of the enfilade contains works by the leading Rococo painter, François Boucher: two small landscapes in the spirit of Watteau, a pastoral, decorative panels made for the prayer chapel of Madame de Pompadour and *a Rest on the Flight into Egypt*. In the centre of the hall is a fine Cupid by the sculptor Etienne-Maurice Falconet, by the walls, next to paintings by François Lemoine and Noël Hallé, are his original plaster models of *The Nymph of a Spring* and a Bather. In the next room on the courtyard side you will find an excellent collection of French applied art from this period.

Etienne Maurice Falconet
(1716–1791)
Sculpture of Flora
Marble
(Hall 285)

François Boucher
(1703–1770)
View in the Environs
of Beauvais. Early 1740s
Oil on canvas. 49 x 58 cm
(Hall 285)

The Display of French
17th–18th-Century Applied Art
(Hall 297)

Cameo Service. 1778–79
Sèvres, France
Soft porcelain
(Hall 297)

Items from the Large Green
Service. 1756
Sèvres Porcelain Factory, France
(Hall 294)

Secretaire. Circa 1760
Made by Dubut, Paris
Rosewood inlaid with ivory and
·mother-of-pearl. 144 x 11 x 48 cm
(Hall 295)

T he light-coloured "Portieres of the Gods"
with a fanciful pattern woven at the Gobelins Factory in Paris; furniture with curving
lines and wavy surfaces decorated with rocaille
ornament; pottery and porcelain in the cases... All
this gives a picture not only of the different forms
of French applied art in the mid 1700s, but also
of the character of a decorative ensemble as a
whole – a Rococo interior.

Of particular interest here is the early French
porcelain. It was first made at Vincennes on the
outskirts of Paris. Production moved to Sèvres,
near Versailles, in 1756 and the factory there
soon became famous. In this hall you can see
items from the first large service created at Sèvres,
the Green Service that Louis XV presented to
King Frederick V of Denmark and Norway in
1758. It is not known how these pieces ended up
in Russia, but many of the over 1,300 items in the
Hermitage's Sèvres collection were made specially for the Russian court. In 1779, for example, the
factory made to an order from Catherine II the

celebrated Cameo Service – its first ensemble in the Classical style that came back into fashion in the 1770s.

If you return along the courtyard side of the wing towards the Alexander Hall, then in the first rooms you will find magnificent furniture, monumental embroidered panels, fabrics, lace and tapestries in sumptuous flowery frames – all items in the Louis XIV style, named after the great king who was the epitome of French absolutism. There is also an ebony cupboard looking like a work of architecture that is decorated with precious wood, brass, tin and gilded bronze made by the famous seventeenth-century crafts-man Charles Boule and a series of tapestries de-picting royal residences and court excursions made from cartoons by Charles Le Brun, First Painter to the King.

The halls in the other direction from the Rococo display that you have already seen give an idea of the Louis XVI style. This designation for a Classical style in applied art gets its name from the last French king before the revolution. The revival of Classicism in the late eighteenth cen-tury was in many ways prepared by the realist tendency in the art of the 1750s–60s that em-bodied the Enlightenment's ideals of social equality and personal freedom. We return to the display of French painting in the halls after Fal-conet and Boucher.

Tapestry: May. The Chateau
of Saint-Germain
The King Riding out with Ladies
From the series The Months,
or the Royal Châteaux
Late 17th – early 18th century
Royal Gobelins Factory, Paris
Wool and silk. 318 x 291 cm
(Hall 292)

Wardrobe. Second half
of the 17th century
André-Charles Boulle, Paris
Ebony, gilded bronze
(Hall 292)

Table. Late 17th century
Wood and pink marble
(Hall 292)

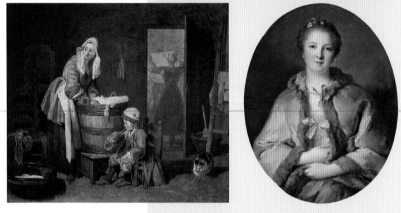

Jean-Baptiste Perroneau
(1715–1783)
Portrait of a Boy with a Book
Mid-1740s
Oil on canvas 63 x 52 cm (Hall 286)

Jean-Baptiste Siméon Chardin
(1699–1779)
Still Life with Attributes
of the Arts. 1766
Oil on canvas 112 x 140.5 cm (Hall 287)

Jean-Baptiste Siméon Chardin
(1699–1779)
A Washerwoman. 1730s.
Oil on canvas 37.5 x 42.7 cm (Hall 287)

Jean-Marc Nattier (1685–1766)
Lady in Grey. 1750s(?)
Oil on canvas. 80 x 64 cm (Hall 286)

Pause in the hall in the centre of which stands a statue of *Winter* by Falconet, executed in the Classical style typical of the sculptor's late work. Here too are sculptural portraits by his gifted pupil and assistant on the *Bronze Horseman* project, Marie-Anne Collot. This hall is devoted to portraiture, a genre that most directly reflected the eighteenth century's characteristic interest in personality, in a person's private world. It gave birth to a new type of formal portrait – the intimate, decorative Rococo portrait, represented here through works by the two of the foremost portraitists of the French court, Jean-Marc Nattier and Louis Tocqué. But the age produced a new kind of buyer and connoisseur of art – the Third Estate that produced the freethinking ideas of the Enlightenment. A notable example of the "Enlightenment" portrait is the *Boy with a Book* by Jean-Baptiste Perroneau, a favourite portraitist of the provincial bourgeoisie. It combines childish

charm with a moral: the book that the serious youngster is holding stands for "the work of childhood" – learning, knowledge.

Affirmation of the ideals of the Third Estate, contrasting them to the emptiness and degeneracy of aristocratic culture, is the basis of "Enlightenment Realism" in art. Its founder was the brilliant painter Jean-Baptiste Chardin. In the next hall are three of his masterpieces. The beauty of inspired work and the morality of ordinary human values – the domestic hearth, the daily concerns of a woman, housewife and mother and everyday utensils turned into a precious image by this "incomparable master of painterly harmony" – link two of his famous genre scenes and a still life.

A direct, although somewhat unimaginative follower of Chardin was Jean-Baptiste Greuze, whose paintings are in the next room. Chardin's influence is also evident in the works of Jean-Honoré Fragonard, the last and greatest painter of the Rococo. The virtuosity of this artist's brush reflects his talent, freedom and temperament. But the growing scale of libertarian ideals in the last years before the 1789 revolution and their social significance that went beyond personal liberty demanded large, universal forms in art. This demand was met by Classicism that manifested itself most powerfully in architecture and sculpture.

France's most outstanding sculptor in the late eighteenth century, Jean-Antoine Houdon, is represented in the Hermitage by a series of remarkable portraits of leading Enlightenment figures and his acknowledged masterpiece – a statue of the great writer and philosopher Voltaire.

The display of French 18th-century art
(Hall 287)

The marble statue of *Voltaire in an Armchair* made to order for Catherine II is Houdon's own replica of the statue that stands in the foyer of the Comédie-Française in Paris.

Jean-Honoré Fragonard (1732–1806). A Stolen Kiss
Late 1780s
Oil on canvas. 45 x 55 cm
(Hall 288)

Jean-Baptiste Greuze (1725–1805)
A Spoilt Child. Early 1760s
Oil on canvas. 66.5 x 56 cm
(Hall 288)

The White Hall. 1838–41
Architect: Alexander Briullov (Hall 289)

Vase. Circa 1786
Sèvres Porcelain Factory
Porcelain with bronze (by Thomire)
Height: 190 cm (Hall 289)

Hubert Robert (1733–1808)
Landscape with a Ruin. 1802
Oil on canvas. 311 x 147 cm (Hall 289)

The display of art by the French Old Masters ends in the White Hall of the Winter Palace. This elegant state room, with moulded compositions and Classical ornament richly covering the walls and vaults as well as a smart fireplace of coloured marbles and jasper, begins the living apartments of Empress Maria Alexandrovna, the wife of Alexander II. They were created by Briullov in 1839–41 for the marriage of Alexander, then still heir to the throne, and Princess Marie of Hesse-Darmstadt. Maria Alexandrovna, as she became, lived here for the rest of her life.

On the walls are large vertical-format canvases that seem part of the decoration of the hall. In actual fact they were painted for a different palace. Their creator was Hubert Robert, an outstanding master of the architectural landscape, painter and decorator of royal parks. One of the last great French artists before the revolution, he did much work to commissions from the Russian nobility. Robert's paintings came into the Hermitage only after 1917, from nationalized private collections and the palaces of the Yusupovs, Stroganovs and Shuvalovs. A series of four paintings including *Landscape with a Ruin* came from the residence of Grand Duke Sergei Alexandrovich, a brother of Alexander III. Robert's "romantic ruins" are the artist's impressions of the countryside and ancient culture of Italy, where he spent ten years as a young man, transformed into decorative canvases with a subtle elegiac mood.

Also of considerable interest in the White Hall are portraits of the Russian aristocracy of Catherine

84

II's time (1762–95) painted by famous French artists. For more than 30 years, the whole length of the Empress's reign, Jean-Louis Voille lived and worked in St Petersburg, producing exquisite female portraits in the sentimental manner then in vogue. The Russian capital gave refuge and success to the portrait-painter to the executed French Queen Marie-Antoinette, Elisabeth Vigée-Lebrun, who is represented by a whole series of works.

The size of the White Hall makes it suitable for the display of monumental works of applied art purchased abroad in the eighteenth century by Russian connoisseurs. For Catherine II the master cabinet-maker David Roentgen produced elaborate desks incorporating secret compartments and clever gadgets, including musical mechanisms. The first consignment of furniture that Roentgen brought from his Paris workshop in 1784 included a mahogany bureau with strict Classical lines adorned by a figure of Apollo. It is one of the craftsman's finest pieces, with a complex mechanical system for opening the inner drawers and compartments. The enormous blue porcelain vase with a grapevine and putti of unglazed biscuit, set in gilded bronze by the celebrated Pierre-Philippe Thomire, was made at the Sèvres factory to a commission from Alexander Bezborodko, a prominent figure of Catherine's reign. At the very end of the eighteenth century the Berlin factory made the porcelain and biscuit table set (a figure of the goddess Flora and vases on legs in the form of satyrs) that King Frederick William of Prussia presented to Alexander I in 1803.

Beyond the White Hall, a masterpiece of Briullov's architecture, comes a succession of rooms that were once Empress Maria Alexandrovna's apartments. Decorated by some of the country's leading nineteenth-century architects, they provide striking examples of the living quarters in the Winter Palace.

Hubert Robert (1733–1808)
Ruins of a Terrace in a Park
Early 1770s
Oil on canvas. 59 x 87 cm (Hall 289)

Jean-Louis Voille
(1744– after 1804)
Portrait of Baroness Stroganova
1781–82
Oil on canvas. 86 x 68.5 cm (Hall 289)

Apollo writing desk. 1783
David Roentgen with Peter
Kinzing. Neuwied, Germany
Mahogany, hornbeam, palisander,
oak, cedar, bronze, brass.

Giovanni Pichler
(1734–1791). Italy
A Centaur
and a Bacchante
Second half
of the 18th century
Sardonyx. 1.7 x 2.4 cm
(Hall 304)

The Geen Dining-Room. 1850s
Architect: Andrei Stakenschneider
(Hall 305)

William Brown (1748–1825)
England. The Head of Hygieia
1785
Cornelian set in gold. 3 x 2.7 cm
(Hall 304)

The classical profile of the Ancient Greek goddess of health Hygieia was carved into a piece of gleaming matte cornelian by the brothers William and Charles Brown, celebrated English masters of glyptic work. The energy of movement and passion marks the depiction of a centaur and bacchante carved from sardonyx by the Italian Giovanni Pichler.

Maria Alexandrovna's state drawing-room is called the Gold Drawing-Room. The name is easily understood as a thin layer of gold leaf entirely covers the walls, doors and moulding on the ceiling, creating an impression of weighty luxury. The interior created by Alexander Briullov was reworked in the 1850s by Andrei Stakenschneider, whom the Empress asked to refurbish her apartments. The room acquired its final appearance and, apparently, the all-over gilding in the 1860s, thanks to the architect Vladimir Schreiber.

It now contains a glyptic collection – carved gems, cameos (with a raised design) and intaglios (with a hollow-cut design) produced by a variety of European schools and craftsmen. Carved from precious or semiprecious minerals, symbols and heraldic devices, portraits and elaborate compositions turned a stone into an amulet, a seal or a keepsake.

The door opposite the windows leads to the cosy Green Dining-Room with false windows, mirrors and painted panels in moulded rocaille frames, an interior in the style of the Rococo, created by Stakenschneider, a master of Historicism (as we have seen in the Small and Old Hermitages).

The Crimson Drawing-Room that follows the Gold was also decorated by Stakenscheider. Its dark-red silk woven with musical notes and instruments (the room was intended for the Empress's musical soirees) suffered badly during the Siege of Leningrad and was restored on the basis of nineteenth-century examples.

As we go away from the grand White Hall, the living apartments get more private and intimate. After the Crimson Drawing-Room comes the exquisite Rococo Boudoir created by Harald Bosse, then the Blue Bedroom that is today used for temporary exhibitions and the adjoining former bathroom decorated with a wave design on the ceiling.

Now we advise you not to grudge the time and return through the French display as far as Lorrain's paintings in order to reach the courtyard-side rooms containing German art of the fifteenth to eighteenth centuries.

The Crimson Drawing-Room
(or Study). Late 1850s
Architect: Andrei Stakenschneider
(Hall 305)

The Crimson Drawing-Room was a place where Empress Maria Fiodorovna would relax and pursue her personal interests – reading, making music, talking with her children and friends. She loved and appreciated art. This room was hung with paintings that belonged to her, including now world-famous Hermitage masterpieces, such as Raphael's *Conestabile Madonna* and Murillo's *Immaculate Conception*. She bequeathed these works to the museum.

The Boudoir. 1853
Architect: Harald Bosse
(Hall 306)

< The Gold Drawing-Room
1860s
Architect: Alexander Briullov
(Hall 304)

Secretaire
Late 16th – early 17th century
Spruce and ash, carved, turned
and inlaid
154 x 129 x 56 cm
(Hall 267)

Ambrosius Holbein
(ca. 1495 – ca. 1520)
Portrait of a Young Man. 1518
Oil and tempera on panel
44 x 32.5 cm
(Hall 264)

Lucas Cranach the Elder
(1472–1553)
Venus and Cupid. 1509
Oil on canvas (transferred from panel
in 1850). 213 x 102 cm
(Hall 264)

The first hall of the display contains the earliest works in which mediaeval art begins to give way to a more realistic treatment of the traditional Christian images. The growing role of the German burgher class, the spread of knowledge and Humanist ideas as well as the influence of the Italian Renaissance gave a strong stimulus to German culture and art at the turn of the sixteenth century. This stage is the most interesting part of the Hermitage collection.

Sadly the painting of the great Dürer is lacking, but in the next room you will encounter some major names of the German Renaissance.

Ambrosius Holbein, the brother of the famous portraitist Hans Holbein the Younger, died young. His portrait of a young man with a face tense with thought against the background of an urban landscape betraying a strong interest in Italian Renaissance architecture is a superb piece of work.

Five paintings by Lucas Cranach the Elder enchant us with their rich colours and the mysterious spirituality of his female images. Cranach organically combined Renaissance Humanism with traditional German mysticism, adding the naïve spirit of the German fairy tale. The slender goddess with the body of an earthly woman in one of the best variants of his celebrated *Venus and Cupid* is both an ideal of beauty and a symbol of sin. The inscription above what is believed to be the first nude in Northern European art reads: "Reject Cupid's

voluptuousness with all your might, or else Venus will possess your blinded soul." Cranach's Virgin beneath a canopy of heavy fruit and the affectedly elegant lady in his *Female Portrait* are full of mystery and symbolic hints, and beautiful as fairy-tale princesses.

The picture of the German Renaissance is expanded by a stained-glass window of the *Lamentation* and a pair of family portraits by the Cologne painter Bartel Bruyn the Elder. Double family portraits were very popular among rich customers from the burgher class who preferred precise likeness and a careful, thorough manner of execution to striking compositions with abundant details. The sole work in the Hermitage by the outstanding artist Adam Elsheimer (1578–1610) is a *St Christopher*.

The works of Jürgen Ovens and Christopher Paudiss date from the 1600s, when German art fell behind the leading European schools.

It flourished again in the second half of the eighteenth century. The excavations of Pompeii in the 1750s that brought antiquity to life and the ideas of the art historian Johann Joachim Winckelmann laid the foundation for Classicism, the main tendency in German art of that era. The work of its exponents – Angelica Kauffmann and the head of German Classicism, Anton Raphael Mengs (the monumental *Perseus and Andromeda*) complete the display of old German art.

Lucas Cranach the Elder
(1472–1553). The Virgin and
Child under the Apple-Tree. 1528
Oil on canvas (transferred
from panel). 87 x 59 cm   (Hall 264)

Anton Raphael Mengs
(1728–1779)
Perseus and Andromeda 1777
Oil on canvas. 227 x 153.5 cm
(Hall 268)

Angelica Kauffmann (1741–1807)
Self-Portrait
Between 1780 and 1785
Oil on canvas. 76.5 x 63 cm   (Hall 268)

The Hall of English Art of the
16th to 17th centuries
(Hall 298)

Thomas Gainsborough
(1727–1788). Portrait of a Lady
in Blue. Late 1770s
Oil on canvas. 76 x 64 cm
(Hall 298)

Josiah Wedgwood (1730–1795)
Items from the Green Frog
Service. 1773–74
Earthenware, overglaze painting
(Hall 300)

Charles (Karl) Kändler (fl. 1720s–
1770s). Wine-Cooler. 1734–35
Cast and chased silver
100 x 169 x 98 cm (Hall 298)

W e pass back through the French halls to
reach the adjoining display of English art.
This opens with portraits from the late
sixteenth and seventeenth centuries. It was with
the portrait that English painting began and foreign artists played the major role at first. Under the
influence of the great Flemish artist Anthony van
Dyck, who worked at the court of Charles I for
almost twenty years, a generation of artists emerged
who laid the foundations for the national school.
The most prominent was Godfrey Kneller, represented by portraits of the sculptor Grinling Gib-
bons and the philosopher John Locke. The English
school reached its brilliant heyday in the eighteenth century, which is epitomized by the works
of famous portraitists – Henry Raeburn, George
Romney and John Hoppner. Shining like a precious gem in this array is a masterpiece by Thomas
Gainsborough – a captivating image, woven from
shades of silvery blue, of an unknown female, who
will always remain *The Lady in Blue*. In this hall it
is impossible to ignore the monumental, opulent
silver wine-cooler weighing over 200 kilos made
by the craftsman Charles Kändler. Applied art
makes up a significant portion of the Hermitage's
English collection. Here and in the neighbouring
halls you can see a selection of English cameos
from the seventeenth and eighteenth centuries,
while the hall after the display of paintings by
Joseph Wright of Derby and George Morland contains the celebrated Green Frog service created
in Josiah Wedgwood's factory in 1770 to a com-

mission from Catherine II for the suburban Chesme Palace. The Finnish name for the palace's locality meant "frog marsh". Hence the little frog featured on each of the 952 items in the creamware service that is decorated with 1,244 views of England. Here too are other products of Wedgwood's experiments in the field of ceramics. On the walls are three paintings by Joshua Reynolds, the historical painter, portraitist and art theoretician who in 1768 became the first president of the Royal Academy. The most famous is *Hercules Strangling the Serpents*, an allegory of emerging Russia painted for Catherine II. Feminine charm and a broad easy manner of painting mark *Cupid Untying the Girdle of Venus*, the artist's replica (made for Prince Potemkin) of his celebrated canvas, for which Emma Hart, later famous as Lady Hamilton, may have posed. The next hall is devoted to nineteenth-century painting. Pride of place here goes to the Romantic formal portraits of Thomas Lawrence, alongside which hang the salon portraits of Christina Robertson, an artist popular in St Petersburg in the early 1800s.

Leave this hall and turn left to pass cases of silverware that end the display of English art. Now we take the wooden stairs to the top floor of the Winter Palace to view the art of France and Europe in the nineteenth and early twentieth centuries.

Joshua Reynolds (1723–1792)
Cupid Untying the Girdle
of Venus. 1788
Oil on canvas 77 x 64 cm (Hall 300)

Thomas Lawrence (1769–1830)
Portrait of Count Mikhail
Vorontsov. 1821
Oil on canvas. 143 x 113 cm (Hall 301)

Joseph Wright of Derby (1734–1797). An Iron Forge Viewed from Without. 1773
Oil on canvas. 105 x 140 cm (Hall 299)

Two-handled goblet with a lid
1726–27
Made by Paul Crespin, London
Cast silver, chased and gilded
Height: 34 cm (Hall 299)

The display of French art of the early 19th century
(Hall of Neo-Classicism)
(Hall 314)

Jacques-Louis David (1748–1825)
Sappho and Phaon. 1809
Oil on canvas. 225.3 x 262 cm (Hall 332)

Jean Antoine Gros (1771–1835)
Napoleon on the Bridge
at Arcola. 1797
Oil on canvas. 134 x 104 cm
(Hall 314)

This painting was inspired by an episode in Napoleon's Italian campaign. Gros was in Milan, and, fascinated with the personality of the general, to whom he was introduced by Josephine Beauharnais, began work on the painting immediately after hearing of his feat on the bridge at Arcola on 16 November 1796. Late that year he made a sketch from life (a chest-length portrait, now in the Louvre); early in 1797 the first version of the painting (now in Versailles) and almost immediately a second – the Hermitage canvas. This was owned by Eugene Beauharnais, Napoleon's stepson, and was brought to Russia by his great-grandson, the Duke of Leuchtenberg.

As you pass through the halls along Palace Square towards the start of the display (the exit from the Cézanne hall to the other staircase), take a look at one of the world's largest and most famous collection of French art from the nineteenth and early twentieth centuries. It begins with the era of the French Revolution and Napoleonic Wars. The hero of the day, General Bonaparte, the future emperor, greets us in Antoine Jean Gros's painting as an inspired warrior rousing his men at the Battle of Arcola. The reality of the subject, the romance of the character and the Classical monumentality of the image all anticipate the complexity and competition of artistic tendencies in nineteenth-century art. Gros has been called a forerunner of Romanticism, yet he was a pupil of Jacques-Louis David, the head of the official Classical school. Other followers of David were François Gérard, who depicted Napoleon's wife Josephine, Pierre-Paul Prud'hon, Pierre-Narcisse Guerin and Anne-Louis Girodet, whose paintings can be seen in the next (courtyard-side) hall together with the museum's only work by David himself. The scrupulous clarity of Classicism soon began to give ground to Romantic passions and

> Théodore Rousseau
(1812–1867)
A Market in Normandy. 1832(?)
Oil on canvas. 29.5 x 38 cm
(Hall 322)

Camille Corot (1796–1875)
Trees in a Marsh
Between 1855 and 1860
Oil on canvas. 25.5 × 38 cm
(Hall 322)

impulses. Although this area of the collection is fairly modest, two masterpieces by the great Romantic Eugène Delacroix, a portrait by Jean-Auguste Ingres, a staunch defender of Classical traditions and David's successor as head of the Academy, and other works give an idea of the clash between the two main tendencies in French art in the early 1800s.

In the middle of the century Classicism, which had degenerated into Salon Academicism (works by Gérôme, Winterhalter, Carolus-Duran, Ziem and others), was opposed by a new trend – Realism. In the Hermitage it is represented by a rich collection of Barbizon-school landscapes. Théodore Rousseau and, following him, Jules Dupré, Diaz de La Peña, Charles-François Daubigny and, close to them in spirit, the dreamy Camille Corot, chose the Fontainebleau forest around the village of Barbizon, not far from Paris, for their experiments in painting outdoors. They pioneered a new method – without preparatory sketches or a drawing as a base, laying paints directly on the canvas to reflect the living colour of nature. This *plein-air* approach would find its logical development in the work of the Impressionists.

< Eugène Delacroix (1798–1863)
A Moroccan Saddling a Horse
1855
Oil on canvas. 56 x 47 cm
(Hall 331)

The exotic East with its colour and mysterious passions stirred Delacroix's imagination. *Moroccan Saddling a Horse is* a late work founded on the artist's memories of a trip to North Africa in 1832. The saddle burns like fire in the Arab's muscular arms; reflections of the sunset gleam in his clothing. The bay horse trembles with impatience, eager to run. A simple subject is transformed into a stirring romantic image.

Claude Monet (1840–1926)
Lady in a Garden (Saint-Adresse). 1867
Oil on canvas. 80 x 99 cm
(Hall 319)

Claude Monet (1840–1926)
Corner of the Garden at
Montgeron 1876–77
Oil on canvas 172 x 193 cm
(Hall 319)

Claude Monet (1840–1926)
Waterloo Bridge (Effect of Fog)
1903
Oil on canvas. 65 x 100 cm
(Hall 319)

Monet's naturally keen perception of colour, refined by
work outdoors, enabled him
to see a multitude of different
shades even on an overcast
day – a task that fascinated
him in his mature years.
In 1899–1901 he travelled
regularly to London, where
from his hotel window he
painted the Thames and its
bridges seen through the
shifting smog.

The two halls after the Barbizon school and Corot contain works by the leading Impressionists Auguste Renoir and Claude Monet. This principal tendency in French art of the 1860s and 1870s acquired its name from Monet's painting *Impression: Sunrise*. Monet was the first to start painting landscapes *en plein-air* and not completing them in the studio, as the Barbizon painters did, but preserving on the canvas the colour dictated by natural light. The white dress of the lady in the garden at Sainte-Adresse (near Le Havre) is painted with dabs of light blue and golden yellow – reflexes from the parasol. Between this early work and the huge canvases painted at Montgeron in the mid-1870s were years of searching and discoveries, poverty and lack of recognition. But the world of flowers, water, wind, cold air and washed-out distances with all its wealth of colour is a triumph of Impressionism. Works belonging to series recording a single motif in different conditions of light and atmosphere – *Haystack, Meadow at Giverny, Poppy Field* and, especially famous, London's *Waterloo Bridge* – give an introduction to Monet's late oeuvre.

For Renoir Impressionism became a means of expressing his theme – life and the essence of contemporary human beings. The young Comédie-Française actress Jeanne Samary is depicted in the brief instant when she stepped from semidarkness and light fell on her face and figure. A single fleeting moment of joy and mild excitement for a young, charming society woman. Yet sooner than others Renoir sensed the limitations of a method that captured only the ephemeral beauty of existence. The Hermitage's Renoirs from the 1880s testify to his pursuit of fullness in his images, returning the graphic element, not as a basis for the application of paints, but as a structure giving them organization. He unites patches of colour "copied" from life into more integral coloured shapes. The rainbow reflections of sunlight from which the sandy path, foliage and figure of a boy are woven come together at the boundaries of the chromatic masses: movement and time have stopped. The image of the boy is no chance moment, but the essence of childhood. In the painting, the model for which was probably Alphonsine Fournaise, the daughter of the owner of La Grenouillere (a restaurant at a bathing spot where Renoir liked to work), large patches in the figure and background, echoed on the open fan, together form an enchanting image of youth and tender reverie, the embodiment of Renoir's ideal of a woman, "beautiful as a flower".

< Claude Monet (1840–1926)
Haystack at Giverny. 1886
Oil on canvas. 61 x 81 cm (Hall 319)

Pierre-Auguste Renoir
(1841–1919)
Child with a Whip. 1885
Oil on canvas. 105 x 75 cm (Hall 320)

Pierre-Auguste Renoir (1841–1919). Portrait of the Actress Jeanne Samary. 1878
Oil on canvas. 174 x 101.5 cm
(Hall 320)

Pierre-Auguste Renoir
(1841–1919)
Girl with a Fan. 1881
Oil on canvas. 65 x 50 cm (Hall 320)

Alfred Sisley (1839–1899)
The Town of Villeneuve-la-
Garenne on the Banks
of the Seine. 1872
Oil on canvas. 59 x 80.5 cm
(Hall 319)

Alfred Sisley. 1839–1899
Windy Day at Véneux.1882
Oil on canvas.. 60 x 81 cm
(Hall 318)

Camille Pissarro. (1830–1903)
The Boulevard Montmartre
in Paris. 1897
Oil on canvas. 73 x 92 cm
(Hall 318)

In the late 1890s Pissarro regularly visited Paris, where he created a series of urban landscapes. The view of the Boulevard Montmartre was painted from the high window of a hotel. The street with its huge buildings and the trees along the boulevard, the carriages and crowds of people seem immersed in translucent coloured air; not dissolving in it, but emerging out of it. The noise and bustle of Paris witnessed by the Impressionist in the spring of 1897 come alive in his canvas.

In the same hall as Monet's paintings, there are works by Alfred Sisley, one of the "lesser" Impressionists. Born in Paris to English parents, Sisley was neither a leader of the movement nor inventor of the method. His art seems intimate and highly personal. He became friends with Monet and Renoir in his youth and went out with them, mastering *plein-air* painting. The Hermitage's three works by Sisley give an idea of his place within Impressionism – a sense of form indivisible from colour, of logic and fine taste. The years separating the bright, joyful *Town on the Seine* that probably featured in the first Impressionist exhibition of 1874 from the late *Windy Day*, tinged with a subtle sense of sorrow, were a bitter time of lack of recognition and want from which Sisley never escaped.

Another "minor", but celebrated Impressionist, Camille Pissarro, an artist who found his theme in the depiction of the modern city, is represented by two views of Paris. Both paintings are in the next room with the works of Pau Cézanne, and that is no concidence.

Kindly Pissarro helped Cézanne learn the *plein-air* method after he left his native Aix-en-Provence and joined the circle of future Impressionists. But Cézanne went down in history as one of the major figures of Post-Impressionism, a brief period that followed the break-up of Impressionism in 1886. This was a time of great loners, not understood or accepted by contemporaries, who opened up new paths in art.

Eleven paintings by Cézanne span his whole career – from the rare pre-Impressionist *Girl at the Piano*, through his 1870s searches for a style on the basis of Impressionism (*Self-Portrait in a Casquette, Bouquet in a Vase and The Banks of the Marne*), to the world-famous masterpieces created in Provence in the 1880s and 1890s. Cezannne's creation form through colour – the painterly equivalent of fruits and handmade objects (*Still Life with a Blue Tablecloth*), the clear air, hot sun and mountains of Provence, and its people seemingly "cut" from the same material (*Great Pine at Aix, Mont Sainte-Victoire, The Smoker*) in which bubbling life and its eternal greatness combine in a single image of the beauty of the world.

Paul Cézanne (1839–1906)
Still Life with Drapery. Circa 1899
Oil on canvas. 53 x 72 cm
(Hall 318)

Paul Cézanne (1839–1906)
The Great Pine-Tree near Aix.
Late 1890s
Oil on canvas. 72 x 91 cm
(Hall 318)

Paul Cézanne (1839–1906)
The Smoker. Circa 1890–92
Oil on canvas. 92.5 x 73.5 cm
(Hall 318)

Paul Cézanne (1839–1906).
Mont Sainte-Victoire. 1900
Oil on canvas. 78 x 99 cm
(Hall 318)

Vincent van Gogh (1853–1890)
Cottages. 1890
Oil on canvas. 60 x 73 cm (Hall 317)

The thatched peasant cottages rooted in the soil, age-old reliable refuges, have twisted, leaned and slipped and are pressed between the rearing earth and the collapsing sky. And all at once Van Gogh's burning colours have faded, as if the life was draining from them. That is how the artist's tragically, morbidly distorted mind is reflected in one of his last works.

Vincent van Gogh (1853–1890)
Lilac Bush. 1889
Oil on canvas. 72 x 92 cm
(Hall 317)

Van Gogh painted *Lilac Bush* in the garden of the Saint-Rémy sanatorium near Arles after the first attack of a grave mental illness brought on by loneliness, poverty and frenetic work. As soon as he began to recover, Van Gogh again took up the brush. The blooming bush, transformed by the artist's temperamental hand – dishevelled, unkempt, agitated by sun and wind, striving upwards into the cold impenetrable blue of the sky – is a symbol of ineradicable hope, of an unquenched thirst for life.

The creative freedom won by the Impressionists stimulated the emergence of a constellation of talents in the short, perhaps 20-year, era of Post-Impressionism. In the halls beyond Cézanne are works by now-famous names: "Douanier" Rousseau, a modern naïve artist, the Neo-Impressionists Paul Signac and Edmond Cross, the Symbolist Odilon Redon. Outstanding among this group, after Cézanne, are Van Gogh and Gauguin. Of the four Van Goghs in the Hermitage, three were painted in the south of France, at Arles, when he was at the height of his powers. All that the lone self-taught artist had accumulated through stubborn work in his native Holland and in Paris, buoyed up by the discoveries of the Impressionists, came to fruition in Provence, in paintings full of ardent love for the world and people: *The Arena at Arles*, one of his first impressions of the city, *Ladies of Arles*, a symbolic image of the blossoming earth, tended by the hands and spiritualized by the soul of woman, and the superb *Lilac Bush*. The fourth, *Cottages*, is one of Van Gogh's last works, produced in Auvers shortly before his tragic death.

Paul Gauguin (1848–1903)
Tahitian Pastorals. 1893
Oil on canvas. 87.5 x 113.7 cm
(Hall 316)

Paul Gauguin (1848–1903)
Woman Holding a Fruit. 1893
Oil on canvas. 92 x 73 cm
(Hall 316)

Gauguin's paintings are allotted a separate hall. They all date from his most important period, after he travelled in 1891 to Oceania on a commission from the French Ministry of Education to "depict the customs and nature of Tahiti". It proved the "corner of the world untouched by civilization" that Gauguin had long sought and where he at last acquired a sense of unity with nature, the world and people. The warm soil of the tropical island, its cool streams, fantastic flora, dusky, half-naked women and men, and stone idols that come alive at twilight turn into fiery paints "set alight by the tropical sun" and live in his paintings subservient to some mysterious law. A woman, the Eve of that remote paradise, processes slowly holding a fruit heavy and round like her breast or a mother's womb –a symbol of temptation or of life? *Where are you going?* the painting is called in the native language. Coloured surfaces and patches gently emerge and stop still in *Tahitian Pastorals*, bewitched by the sound of the *vivo*, the ancient flute; humans, beasts and nature have all frozen. The artist profoundly sensed "the concord of human, animal and plant life" and conveyed it in the harmony of his paintings.

Paul Gauguin (1848–1903)
Sunflowers. 1901
Oil on canvas. 73 x 92 cm (Hall 316)

Sunflowers is one of Gauguin's last paintings, created on the island of Hiva Oa, where his life ended in lonely obscurity. It is a piece of nostalgia. The mature, nodding flowers may well be a guilty recollection of his dead friend Van Gogh, who decorated their poor lodgings in Arles with images of sunflowers. The light is fading, flaring up in the last bursts of precious colour. From the gloom a stem raises an enormous, all-seeing eye – a reminder of another friend, the painter Odilon Redon. The mysterious face in the window – of a native or the Buddha? – is the inscrutable countenance of Polynesia, the "promised land, tropical paradise" that gave a brief moment of harmony and joy.

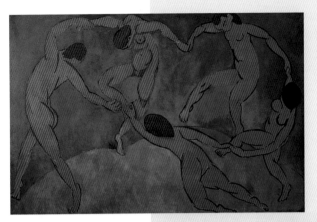

Henri Matisse
(1869–1954)
The Dance. 1910
Oil on canvas
270 x 391 cm
(Hall 344)

Henri Matisse (1869–1954)
Moroccan Woman (Zorah). 1912
Oil on canvas. 146 x 61 cm   (Hall 345)

Henri Matisse (1869–1954)
Spanish Still Life
Circa 1910–11
Oil on canvas. 89.5 x 116.3 cm
(Hall 345)

T he halls beyond Gauguin are devoted to French art of the early 1900s. The Hermitage has world-famous collections of two great twentieth-century artists – Henri Matisse and Pablo Picasso. The 37 paintings by Matisse date from the most important period in his career, the time of Fauvism, the first avant-garde movement of the new century of which he was head, and the formation of his monumental style of painting. From early chromatic experiments in still lifes and landscapes, the display leads up to the triumph of colour in the celebrated canvases of 1907–14. Matisse's colour is not a reflection of the colourfulness of the world, but an expression of its essence, a sign of truth and beauty. The colourfulness of objects in the *Seville Still Life* becomes in the *Spanish Still Life* a generalized chromatic symbol of the beauty of human existence and does so with the even greater power of a "solo performance" in *The Red Room*. The blue and green in the famous panels *Dance* and *Music*, the fire of the red bodies caught up in a furious "farandole" or disintegrating into immobile patches with black openings for eyes and mouths giving out sound are symbols of the earth, sky and the human creative urge.

Pablo Picasso (1881–1973)
Violin and Guitar. 1913
Oil on canvas. 65 x 54 cm
(Hall 348)

Pablo Picasso (1881–1973)
Jug in the form
of a woman's head
Ceramic. Height: 37 cm
(Hall 348)

The painter found his own chromatic harmony to convey the (for Europeans) mysterious beauty of the East in works painted under the influence of a journey to Morocco in 1912–13.

Spanish-born Picasso, who spent all his adult life in France, spoke of the most important and universal things in the contemporary world using his own language of painterly construction. Over 30 of the best early works from his Blue (*The Visit, The Absinthe-Drinker*), Pink and Cubist periods give an idea of the creative searchings of his youth. Picasso was the founder and chief exponent of Cubism, a method of bringing out the constructional essence of objects and figures. By removing their fleshly wrappings, the artist lays bare the truth of the natural mechanisms of human characters and phenomena (*Woman with a Fan, Peasant Woman, Woman with a Mandolin*). From diverse elements he "synthesizes" a new object, a new world, the world of music, for example, made up of fragments of instruments and notes or a collage of wallpaper, sand and sawdust.

Pablo Picasso (1881–1973)
The Absinthe Drinker. 1901
Oil on canvas. 73 x 54 cm
(Hall 348)

Pablo Picasso (1881–1973)
Woman with a Fan
(After the Ball). 1908
Oil on canvas. 152 x 101 cm
(Hall 348)

Picasso developed an interest in ceramics after the Second World War. The ceramic works in the display are testimony to the insatiable urge to experiment and create that remained with him to the end of his life.

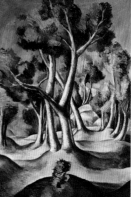

Maurice de Vlaminck
(1876–1958)
Town on the Shore of a Lake
Circa 1909
Oil on canvas. 81.3 x 100.3 cm
(Hall 347)

André Derain (1880–1954)
The Grove. 1912
Oil on canvas. 116 x 81 cm
(Hall 347)

Kees van Dongen (1877–1968)
Lady in a Black Hat. Circa 1908
Oil on canvas. 100 x 81.5 cm
(Hall 347)

Along with Matisse and Picasso, the early-twentieth-century avant-garde is represented in the Hermitage by a wide range of the most notable artists who lived and worked in Paris, the artistic capital of the world at that time, whose very atmosphere seemed to encourage freedom, searches and discoveries. The first such discovery was Fauvism and the display contains works by all its chief exponents – those whose glaring, unrestrained colours in works displayed at the 1905 Salon d'Automne earned them the epithet *fauves* ("wild beasts") from one critic. The group, bound together by their common experiment (a "trial by fire", as André Derain put it), soon broke up as each artist went his own way.

Maurice Vlaminck remained a loner, an artist whose landscapes are always dominated by dramatic emotion. His friend Derain, with whom he shared ideas and a studio in suburban Chatou, turned in 1908 to Cubism, which proved closer to his constructional perception of nature and French passion for logical expression. The 14 paintings by Derain in the Hermitage reveal the range of his talent – portraits, landscapes and still lifes, all with a strikingly powerful plastic structure, formed by rigid boundaries of light and dark from the dense painterly material. The Dutchman Kees van Dongen devoted his Fauvist experience, provocative brush and sultry palette to the artistic Bohemia of Montmartre, an artificial world of screaming colours and wickedly beautiful *femmes fatales*, a world in the depth of which one senses thoughts of the sadness and gloominess of life. The Fauvist experiment also lay behind the refined idiom of Albert Marquet's intimate landscapes and the decorative virtuosity of Raoul Dufy's painting.

ul Dufy (1877–1953)
atta (Sailing Ships in the Harbour
Deauville). Circa 1936
in canvas. 54 x 80.8 cm (Hall 350)

A variety of early twentieth-century artistic trends can be found in the last hall of the French display. There are the near-abstract compositions of Amedée Ozenfant and Fernand Léger, a modern classic who began with Cubism and created his own painterly system, the main theme of which is the beauty and harmony of the modern world, transformed by technical thinking. There are also the works of the Montmartre painter Maurice Utrillo that continue the *plein-air* tradition and the canvases, each tragic in its own way, of the Expressionists Georges Rouault and Chaim Soutine.

These last are relatively recent acquisitions, bought at auction in Paris in 1998, but the overwhelming majority of the works from the Impressionists onwards are the legacy of two celebrated turn-of-the-twentieth-century Muscovite collectors and connoisseurs: Sergei Shchukin and Ivan Morozov. It is to their collecting passion, taste and knowledge that the Hermitage owes one of the world's best collections of French art from the second half of the nineteenth century and beginning of the twentieth.

Albert Marquet (1875–1947)
Marina (Naples). 1909
Oil on canvas. 61.5x 80 cm
(Hall 350)

Maurice Utrillo (1883–1955)
The Rue Custine in Montmartre
1909–10
Oil on cardboard. 52 x 71 cm
(Hall 350)

Fernand Léger (1881–1955)
Carte Postale
Oil on canvas. 92 x 65 cm
(Hall 350)

Caspar David Friedrich
(1774–1840)
On a Sailing Ship. 1818–19
Oil on canvas. 71 x 56 cm

(Hall 342)

The Hermitage has nine paintings by Friedrich that were acquired in the 1820s by Nicholas I (before his accession) on the recommendation of the Russian Romantic poet Zhukovsky. The best of them, *On a Sailing-Ship* was bought directly from the artist's studio. The ship with the wind full in its sails carrying a pair of lovers to hazy sunlit shores is a romantic image, a symbol of a joint voyage over the "sea of life" towards a bright goal. The work was painted soon after Friedrich's honeymoon trip to the North German island of Rügen which provided some of his favourite motifs for painting.

We are back on the landing of the Wooden Staircase. From here we follow the windows overlooking the courtyard of the Winter Palace to the first hall in the display of nineteenth-century German art. This is a fairly small collection, but nonetheless rates as one of the best outside Germany itself.

The first hall contains works by one of the most celebrated German Romantic artists, Caspar David Friedrich. His paintings gave profound expression to the characteristic moods of German Romanticism – nostalgia, a longing for what is lost, unattainable or enigmatically beautiful. Nature has the leading role in Friedrich's work; it creates a special atmosphere of quiet, pensive mystery. Enveloped in fogs and dissolving in the endless skies, the snow-covered peaks of the Riesengebirge mountains above empty valleys (highland landscapes were one of Friedrich's favourite motifs) turn into an image of the almost threatening, mystic boundlessness of the universe. Also lost amongst nature in Friedrich's paintings are the human figures – aloof observers lost in a stupor of hopeless melan-

choly, a yearning for pipe dreams, and the silhouettes of ships and old Gothic buildings melting in a glistening hazy light.

Withdrawal into the past, a fascination with the Middle Ages is another characteristic feature of Romanticism that found vivid expression in the works of the Düsseldorf school. In the first large work by Karl Friedrich Lessing, the foremost member of the school, a real-life event – the death of a young girl – acquired the look of a mediaeval tale, echoing a ballad by the Romantic poet Ludwig Uhland. Romanticism in Germany was more than just the dominant artistic tendency in the first half of the nineteenth century, it was a worldview, aesthetic and philosophy that continued to inspire German art even when it later began to subscribe to other systems and ideals. We can sense its "intonation" in the depiction of the inner courtyard of the royal residence in Munich by the Symbolist Hans von Marées, and even in *Girl in a Field*, a landscape painted by Ludwig Knaus under the influence of the Barbizon school – works in the following hall. The Romantic attitude also tints German portraiture in this period, even the formal depictions of Franz Krüger, the official artist of the Russian court. Anselm Feuerbach, the nephew of the philosopher, depicted himself as a true "Romantic hero" with a mysterious dash of the infernal in his self-portrait. Feuerbach was known in Karlsruhe as Fra Diavolo after a well-known opera character following his return from a long period in Paris and Italy.

Anselm Feuerbach (1829–1880)
Self-Portrait
Oil on canvas. 92 x 73 cm (Hall 341)

Franz Krüger (1797–1857)
Portrait of Prince Nikolai
Saltykov in Fancy Dress. 1850
Oil on canvas. 98 x 79 cm
(Hall 342)

The portrait of Nikolai Ivanovich Saltykov, depicting the young Russian aristocrat in a striking pose in front of a Romantic landscape, is one of Krüger's best works in the Hermitage. In all the museum has twelve – battle scenes, military parades and portraits. Krüger, the court painter of the Prussian King Frederick William III, was invited to Russia by Nicholas I, whose favourite artist he was.

< Caspar David Friedrich (1774–1840). The Riesengebirge Mountains
Oil on canvas. 73.5 x 102.5 cm
(Hall 342)

< Karl Friedrich Lessing (1808–1880)
The Royal Couple Mourning the Death of Their Daughter. 1830
Oil on canvas. 215 x 193 cm (Hall 342)

Wassily Kandinsky (1866–1944)
Russia, Germany
Composition No 6. 1913
Oil on canvas. 194 x 294 cm
(Hall 334)

Kandinsky's "compositions" are the most consistent embodiment of his principle of non-figurative painting. In *Composition No 6*, one of the most significant in the series, the artist's starting-point was the biblical Flood. But rather than the event, it was the complex, obscure, powerful state of mind and spirit – the "inner necessity", as Kandinsky called it – that he conveyed on the canvas in a free arrangement of coloured lines and patches with an overall headlong rhythm and deep blue tone – the colour of cold waters, skies and eternity. The result is a grand, powerful symphony of colour, "a song of praise, a hymn of rebirth following death".

Alexei von Jawlensky (1864–1941). Russia, Germany
Landscape with a Red Roof
1910s
Oil on canvas. 53 x 32 cm
(Hall 334)

Twentieth-century German art is represented by a small circle of works. Notable among them are a painting by the major Symbolist Franz von Stuck, *Fight over a Woman*, created under the influence of the teachings of the philosopher Friedrich Nietzsche, and two examples of Expressionism, the chief tendency in German art in the first decades of the century, by Heinrich Emsen and Heinrich Campendonck. These were transferred to the Hermitage in 1948, when the authorities closed the Museum of New Western Art in Moscow, together with paintings from the collections of Shchukin and Morozov, and a number of works of modern art. That is how the Hermitage acquired five paintings by one of the main creators of abstract art, the Russian painter Wassily Kandinsky. They are among his first non-figurative canvases, created in Germany in the 1910s. At that time the artist was head of the famous Blauer Reiter group of Expressionists in Munich, which included his friend Alexei Jawlensky (also represented in the display). Alongside Kandinsky's

< Kazimir Malevich (1878–1935)
Russia. Black Square. 1929–30(?)
Oil on canvas. 53.5 x 53.5 cm (Hall 334)

Diego Maria Rivera (1886–1957)
Mexico
Still Life. 1913
Tempera on canvas. 84 x 65 cm
(Hall 334)

Rockwell Kent (1882–1957)
USA
Admiralty Gulf. 1922
Oil on canvas. 86 x 112 cm (Hall 334)

Fernando Botero (Born 1932)
Columbia
Still Life with Watermelon
1976–77
Bronze (Hall 334)

paintings is the *Black Square*, a replica by the Russian artist Kazimir Malevich, the founder of geometrical abstraction, of his own celebrated painting. This is one of the Hermitage's first acquisitions of modern art (made in 2002), something that has now become possible. But the museum collection does not give a comprehensive picture of art outside Russia after 1917. It formed in the Soviet era from chance acquisitions of individual works by artists from various countries: Hungary, Poland, Romania, the USA, Canada and Latin America. From the 1960s the collection grew through gifts made by famous artists. In 1964 the American Rockwell Kent donated several landscapes painted in Greenland and Canada. Major figures who had exhibitions in the Hermitage presented works. That is how the museum gained paintings by the leading French abstractionist Pierre Soulages and a sculptural composition by the distinguished Columbian arts Fernando Botero. Gifts also make up a considerable part of the collection of Italian twentieth-century art kept at the end of the courtyard-side display.

This sculptural piece consisting of rounded objects that seem to be swelling out of the mass of metal forcing them apart and lying on an equally massive table may be an ironic paraphrasing of the classical still life as seen in Dutch "breakfasts" or perhaps an image of sleepy, self-satisfied everyday existence, or even the magic of mysterious forces embodied in the immobility of heavy rigid forms. This is a very typical work by the major contemporary Columbian artist Fernando Botero, who has a close kinship with naïve art of the grotesque-traditionalist tendency.

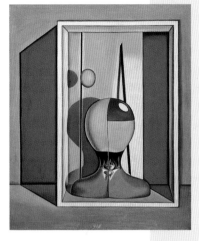

Giorgio Morandi (1890–1964)
Still Life. 1920s
Oil on canvas. 51 x 57.5 cm
(Hall 337)

Giorgio Morandi (1890–1964)
Metaphysical Still Life. 1918
Oil on canvas. 71.5 x 61.5 cm
(Hall 337)

Francesco Messina (1900–1995)
Beatrice. 1959. Bronze. Heigt: 145 cm
(Hall 335)

The collection of twentieth-century Italian art is not large and does not give a complete picture of artistic life in the country in that period. Still, the individual works that have come into the museum allow us to feel the tense pulse of Italian artists' searchings in that complex era. At the start of the century Italy produced Futurism and Metaphysical Art – two major tendencies that played an important role in the development of art. Although the Hermitage lacks works by Futurists or Giorgio de Chirico, the creator of Metaphysical Painting, Giorgio Morandi's *Metaphysical Still Life* eloquently testifies to Italian creative strivings in the early 1900s. The absolute purity of lines and geometrical forms reveals the super-sensual metaphysical – beyond the bounds of reality – essence of an image extracted, it was believed, from the depths of the unconscious. Just two paintings by Morandi nonetheless allow us to assess him, not only as kindred spirit to Chirico and forerunner with him of the Surrealists, but also as a great painter, a contemplator and refined colourist, who penetrated deeply into the beauty and mystery of things. Several decades separate Morandi's paintings from the works of Renato Guttuso, another bright figure in Italian twentieth-century art, the creator and leader of Neo-Realism, the leading trend in the country's art after the Second World War. Between these two "landmarks", there are only a few works from the 1920s and 1930s, by Pompeo Borra, Filippo de Pisisa and Massimo Campigli, but they can give us an idea of efforts to

108

create new art by reviving and transforming in the modern context the classical traditions of the once-great Italian school. This is especially evident in sculpture, which is very well represented in the museum. In the early 1980s the Hermitage received a series of gifts from leading Italian sculptors. It would be hard not to appreciate the vivid plastic quality of the still not fully formed young body of *Beatrice*, with an enchanting almost Classical harmony of proportions and pure lines, in the work by the major Realist Francesco Messina. Classical nobility and monumentality of sculptural forms combined with modern freedom and dynamism link Messina with the works of the outstanding monumentalist Emilio Greco, the lyrical sculptor Augusto Murer, and one of the boldest innovators, the celebrated artist Giacomo Manzu. He gave the Hermitage several of his works: two reliefs on the theme of the *Crucifixion* (a favourite vehicle for the expression of his innermost feelings and thoughts, that established itself in his art in the 1930s under the very strong impression of the reliefs on the portal of San Zeno Maggiore in Verona) and two sculptures and a painting linked by the theme of "the artist and model", a key one in Manzu's oeuvre: he "voices" the dialogue between them as he recreates her before our eyes from paints or heavy, gleaming bronze.

We now leave the display of the Western European department. From the upper landing of the Wooden Staircase, we move on to the halls of the Department of the East.

Renato Guttuso (1912–1987)
Portrait of Rocco and His Son
1960
Oil on canvas. 136 x 113 cm
(Hall 337)

Giacomo Manzu (1908–1990)
Tebe Sitting. 1983
Bronze. Height: 125 cm
(Hall 337)

Giacomo Manzu (1908–1990)
Crucifixion
Relief. Bronze. 68.5 x 49.5
(Hall 336)

The he world of the East in the Hermitage is huge: over 180,000 exhibits in 78 halls present the culture and art of all parts of the East from ancient times to the twentieth century. Here, on the top floor of the Winter Palace, are the displays of the Far and Middle East.

The items in the first hall from the staircase – traditional *guo hua* (ink on paper) painting, carved furniture, cloisonné enamel elephants, a Coromandel lacquer screen with scenes of court life, birds and flowers – take us into the realm of Chinese art. This is not the beginning but the end of an immense display that covers almost 2,500 years of its history. Moving through the halls with windows overlooking the courtyard, you will see above all applied art, pieces that astonish with their imagination, exquisite style and superb workmanship. China's famous porcelain is represented mainly by items from its greatest period, the 1600s and 1700s: dishes and plates painted in five colours (*famille verte* – strong green, iron red, yellow, purple and violet blue) or six colours (*famille rose* with the addition of pink and carmine introduced from Europe) with depictions of fish, butterflies, birds, flowers and fruit; cobalt bowls and figurines of fantastic beasts. Tables, boxes, incense burners and pots decorated with esoteric meaning demonstrate traditional Chinese materials and techniques – carved lacquer, wood, stone (items made from translucent jade are especially typical) and ivory.

Continuing, you enter a hall containing unique exhibits from the ancient city of Khara-Khoto, the capital of a Tangut state that existed in the Gobi desert from 982 to 1227. The sand-covered site

Screen with flowers and birds and scenes from the life of the imperial court. 12 panels. China
Wood, mineral paints,
Coromandel lacquer. 280 x 720 cm
(Hall 357)

Figure of an elephant. China,
Yung-cheng period (1723–35)
Cloisonné enamel (Hall 357)

< Dish. China, Kangxi period
(1662–1772)
Porcelain, polychrome overglaze
painting (Hall 356)

< The Pure Land of the Amida
Buddha. Khara-Khoto, Tibet
Natural paints on canvas
99 x 63.8 cm (Hall 353)

was discovered and studied by the famous traveller
Piotr Kozlov in the early twentieth century. The
greatest treasures here are Tibeto-Tangut and Chinese Buddhist images executed on paper, silk and
canvas, including a masterpiece portrait of a gar-
dener. The last halls before the Saltykov Staircase
contain the earliest items of Chinese Buddhist art
in the Hermitage – fifth- to tenth-century works
from the Cave of the Thousand Buddhas monastery (Ch'ien-fo Tung) discovered in the early 1900s
near Tun-huang. More Buddhist art awaits, if you
go back from the Saltykov Staircase along the windowless gallery – painting and sculpture from the
monasteries of the Sinkiang region of north-west
China and in the parallel enfilade the art of Tibet
from the eighth century onwards. At the end of
this enfilade are monumental portraits of noble
Chinese from the sixteenth century.

From here you can enter the display of Indian
art, where you will see great works of sculpture in
stone and bronze, precious fabrics, weapons and
the celebrated Mughal miniatures of the seventeenth and eighteenth centuries. Then, to continue
your acquaintance with the Department of the
East, you need to return to the Saltykov Staircase.

Guhyamantrayana. 18th century
Tibet
Gilded bronze. Height: 24 cm

Unknown artist
Portrait of an Official
11th–12th century
Khara-Khoto, China
India ink on paper. 45 x 31.8 cm
(Hall 352)

Head of a Bohisattva
8th century. Tun-huang
(Dunhuang), China
Clay, natural paints. Height: 37 cm
(Hall 351a)

Maithuna lovers
8th–10th century. India
Sandstone. Height: 70 cm (Hall 370)

Triptych depicting the Forty
Martyrs on the lake of Sebaste.
10th–11th century. Byzantium
Carved and painted ivory with silver
18.5 x 24.2 cm (Hall 383)

Icon of Christ the Pantocrator
Circa 1363. Byzantium
Tempera on panel (limewood)
106 x 79 x 2.8 cm (Hall 383)

Dish bearing a depiction
of Shapur II out hunting
4th century. Sassanid Iran
Chased silver. Diameter: 22.9 cm
(Hall 383)

The dish bearing a depiction
of King Shapur II out hunting is
one of the best-known pieces
of Sasanid silver. The galloping
horseman draws his bow to
shoot a fierce lion that is depicted twice – fighting for its
life and defeated. The skill of a
craftsman, who superbly inscribed the dynamic composition in a tight circle, and a
wealth of finely worked details
make this a truly "royal" piece
of work.

On the other side of the Saltykov Staircase
is the Near and Middle Eastern display.
The first halls contain the collection of art
from Byzantium, a powerful mediaeval Christian
state in the Balkans and the eastern Mediterranean.
The display gives a picture of Byzantine art
throughout its thousand-year history, from the
fourth-century to the fall of the empire in 1453.
Applied art is represented in all its variety of techniques and forms: silver vessels, lead seals, cloisonné enamels, carved ivory. Among the masterpieces
are a silver paten, an ivory diptych (two panels
hinged together) from the fifth century with circus
scenes and a tenth- or eleventh-century triptych
with depictions of forty martyrs. The pride of the
collection, though, is the group of Byzantine icons.
Such outstanding works as *St Gregory the Miracle-
Worker and Christ Pantocrator* give a profound
sense of the beauty of the Byzantine spiritual world
as embodied in art.

After Byzantium comes a large display of the
culture and art of Iran. It begins with works from
the era of the Sasanids, a dynasty that created a
state on Iranian territory in the third century. There
are extremely rare examples of the celebrated Sasanid silver, with over 100 items the best collection
outside Iran – precious vessels bearing scenes of
hunting, fabulous beasts and deities that once
adorned the daily lives of Sasanid nobles. The absolute proof of the authenticity of these objects is the
fact that they were found in ancient hoards in the
Russian North, on the line of age-old trade routes.

This art did not disappear with the Arab conquest
in the seventh century. Revitalized by Muslim traditions, it was reborn in mediaeval Iranian bronze as
can be seen in the following halls. Here is the famous

Bronze aquamanile
in the shape of a zebu cow
1206. Ali ibn Muhammad ibn
Abu-l-Qasim, Iran
Cast bronze inlaid with silver
Height: 35 cm (Hall 384)

aquamanile (water jug) in the form of a zebu cow
being attacked by a snow leopard as it feeds its calf
and a kettle from Herat inlaid with an Arabic inscription and figures of horsemen and musicians.

Iranian ceramics are represented by a superb
thirteenth-century lustre vase from Kashan show-
ing a game of polo and faience from Isfahan, Ker-
man, Yazd and Meshed. Plus carpets from Isfahan
and Tabriz, fabrics, weapons... Among the works of
Iranian painting on display your attention will
probably be attracted by the formal portraits from
the early-nineteenth-century reign of Fath-Ali
Shah that combine European oil-painting technique with traditional forms of Muslim art.

The next halls contain one after another displays from the countries of the Islamic East, Arabic
Egypt, Iraq, Syria – note the bronzes, fabrics, ceramics and especially the glass and rock-crystal
vessels – real Aladdin's lamps!

The halls of the art and culture of the once-
mighty Ottoman (Turkish) Empire, containing pottery from Iznik and other centres, carpets, gold
braid and weapons, complete the displays from
the Near and Middle East.

We now go down the Saltykov Staircase to the
ground floor of the Winter Palace, where we will
visit the ancient artefacts of the Department of
Archaeology.

Vase bearing a depiction of a
game of polo. 13th century. Iran
Earthenware with lustre glaze
Height: 80 cm (Hall 387)

Kettle. 1163. Herat, Iran
Cast and raised bronze (brass) with
silver and copper inlay. Height: 18.5 cm
(Hall 384)

Mihr-Ali. Portrait of Fath Ali Shah
Iran. 1809–10
Oil on canvas. 253 x 124 cm (Hall 393)

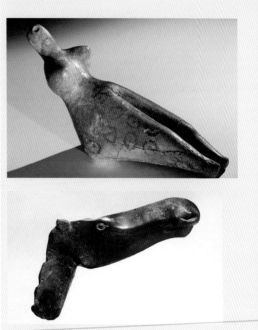

The display of the Department of Archaeology. The Gothic Drawing-Room. 1838–39
Architect: Alexander Briullov (Hall 12)

Statuette of a seated womanAeneolithic (Copper Age) Second half of the 4th century B.C. Found at Yalangach-Depe, Southern Turkmenia
Earthenware. Length: 27 cm (Hall 12)

Head of a doe-elk
2nd millennium B.C. Urals
Horn. Length: 19.5 cm
(Hall 13)

The horn sculpture of a doe-elk's head found in the Shigirsky peat-bog was executed with striking precision, a knowledge and understanding of the animal, yet without unnecessary detail. The generalized forms give it a symbolic meaning; the faultless purity of line gives it a finished aesthetic beauty. All in all this little work of sculpture (used a handle or the top of a staff) is a masterpiece of ancient art.

The corridor we have entered and the rooms on each side contain the displays of the Department of the Archaeology of Eastern Europe and Siberia. Created in 1931, it possesses around 400,000 artefacts of ancient cultures spanning a period from the Stone Age to the early Middle Ages. Take the corridor to the left of the door from which we have just come, past the Church Staircase to the security desk, next to which is the entrance to the first halls of the display. Before the revolution, these were the rooms of the imperial children. The Gothic Drawing-Room (Alexander Briullov, 1838–39) and the pseudo-Rococo Hall with Cupids (Andrei Stakenschneider, 1856) have retained their décor from that time. On show here are the oldest Stone Age artefacts – earthenware, primitive stone and bone tools, and some of the earliest works of human art – bone figurines and ornamented plaques from an ancient campsite close to Irkutsk; petroglyphs (boulders with outlines of animals, birds and hunters cut into them) from Lake Onega; clay statuettes of women, examples of plastic art from the sixth to third millennia B.C. produced by the agricultural cultures of southern Turkmenistan, Ukraine and Moldova. Here too are well-known archaeological complexes: the Neolithic settlement discovered in 1914 in a peat bog in Yeketerinburg region (the Urals);

114

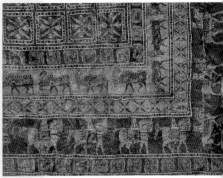

Chariot. 5th–4th century B.C.
5th Pazyryk burial mound, Pazyryk,
Altai mountains, Southern Siberia
Wood and leather. Height: 300 cm
(Hall 25)

Swan. 5th–4th century B.C.
5th Pazyryk burial mound, Pazyryk,
Altai mountains, Southern Siberia
Felt Length: 29 cm (Hall 26)

Bronze Age artefacts from the Maikop burial mound (mid-third millennium B.C.) and the Koban Culture of the northern Caucasus (eleventh to eight centuries B.C.). The halls with windows facing the Admiralty hold works representing the culture and art of the Scythians, a nomadic people that lived in the area north of the Black Sea in the seventh to third centuries B.C. There are bronze vessels, arms and harness from burial mounds. The famous Scythian gold is kept separately in the Treasure Gallery.

Emerging from the last hall and crossing the same corridor as before, we enter a hall that contains artefacts of the peoples of southern Siberia that are unique in both style and state of preservation. Pazyryk in the Altai Mountains, once the burial site of tribal chiefs, yielded items of perishable materials preserved by permafrost. Wooden, leather and felt ornaments in the Animal style; a huge felt carpet with coloured appliqué patches made locally; a wooden burial chariot; the world's oldest Eastern pile carpet and Chinese silks create an exceptionally fine picture of the ancient lifestyle of nomadic peoples. After this brief visit to the Department of Archaeology we return once more to the Saltykov Staircase and go up one floor, to the displays of the Department of the History of Russian Culture.

Pile carpet. Detail. 5th–4th century B.C. 5th Pazyryk burial mound, Pazyryk, Altai mountains, Southern Siberia
Wool. 200 x 185 cm (Hall 25)

Carpet. 5th–4th century B.C.
5th Pazyryk burial mound, Pazyryk, Altai mountains, Southern Siberia
Coloured felt, appliqué. 4.5 x 6.5 metres
(Hall 26)

The pile carpet from Pazyryk is almost a thousand years older than the most ancient Persian carpets, but it was created using the same hand-knotting technique, with 3,600 knots to every decimetre. Its colour and pattern (ornamental stripes and a procession of animals) are on a par with the best Eastern carpets.

Bartolomeo Carlo
Rastrelli (1675–1744)
Bust of Peter the Great
1723–29
Bronze. Height: 102 cm (Hall 158)

Ship goblet. 1706
St Petersburg
Cast, chased, engraved
and gilded silver
30.5 x 12 x 37 cm (Hall 161)

The Rotunda
Early 1830s; 1838–39
Architects: Auguste Montferrand;
Alexander Briullov
(Hall 156)

Copying Lathe. 1729
Andrei Nartov (1693–1756)
St Petersburg
Height: 228.5 cm (Hall 161)

Turning left after leaving the staircase, we walk along the Dark Corridor (hung with eighteenth-century Western European tapestries) and enter the Rotunda.

This perfectly round room beneath a high dome, created by Auguste Montferrand and restored by Alexander Briullov after the 1837 fire, links several suites of former living rooms that now contain the displays of the Department of the History of Russian Culture.

The department, created in 1941, has over 300,000 items dating from the fifth century onwards. These are mainly works of applied art, archaeological materials, scientific and technical items, weapons and banners, as well as works of fine art, mainly of historical significance.

From the Rotunda we enter the suite of rooms to the left of the Dark Corridor – the display of Russian culture of the first quarter of the eighteenth century, the time of Peter the Great. The cases in the first hall contain prints by the craftsmen of the engraving studio that Peter founded – the Dutchman Adriaen Schoonebeck and the Russian artist Alexei Zubov that record the appearance of St Petersburg, the new city that Peter founded in 1703 and made his capital in 1712, the launching of a ship of the young Russian navy and festive gather-

ings. Navigational and medical instruments, a goblet in the form of a ship that was cast from the first silver mined in Transbaikalia to mark a Russian naval victory in the Baltic, and many other items in the following halls give a picture of the wide-ranging cultural changes of the era. One of the masterpieces of the collection is a bronze bust of Peter I by the sculptor Carlo Bartolomeo Rastrelli, the father of the architect of the Winter Palace. Paintings by foreign artists that the Tsar invited to Russia and the Russian artists Andrei Matveyev and Ivan Nikitin, whom Peter sent abroad to learn the basics of European painting, tell of the birth of a new artistic school in Russia.

The Petrine era was a time when a new national culture of a European type formed in this country. The merging of Russian and European traditions shaped the look of the urban home of Peter's day, which is recreated in the display: a table with a painted top made by Arkhangelsk craftsmen; chairs with high backs of Dutch and English types, on the wall the first Russian tapestry, *The Battle of Poltava*, woven by the Frenchman Philippe Behagle and his Russian apprentice Kobyliakov at the factory Peter established in St Petersburg.

The image of Peter himself, the reformer tsar, the "constant worker on the throne", is resurrected by articles, many of which were his personal possessions, kept after his death (until 1848) in the Kunstkammer, the first Russian museum, which he founded: a copying lathe made specially for a man of Peter's great height (2.04 metres) and improved by Andrei Nartov, one of his protégés; a chandelier and other items made of walrus ivory and wood in Peter's turnery with his direct participation; a campaign medicine chest, formal and working clothes.

The Display of Russian Culture of the First Quarter of the Eighteenth Century (Hall 159)

Ivan Nikitin (1680s–1742)
Portrait of Empress Elizabeth as a Child. Circa 1712
Oil on canvas. 54 x 43 cm
(Hall 166)

The European technique of painting in oils is combined with a spirituality and sincere emotionality in keeping with the traditions of old Russian icon-painting in the depiction of a child, one of the earliest Russian works of portraiture, created by Ivan Nikitin.

Peter the Great's Campaign Medicine Chest. Circa 1613–15
Augsburg, Germany
Wood, metal and glass with oil painting on copper and gilding
39.5 x 41 x 32.5 cm (Hall 166)

Ivan Vishniakov (1699–1761)
Portrait of Stepanida Yakovleva
After 1756
Oil on canvas. 90 x 72 cm (Hall 163)

Alexei Antropov (1716–1795)
Portrait of Fiodor Dubiansky
1761
Oil on canvas. 99.5 x 76.5 cm (Hall 163)

The portrait of Empress Elizabeth's chaplain Archpriest Dubiansky is one of Alexei Antropov's finest works.
The solemn immobility, the imperious pose and gestures convey the will, intelligence and spiritual strength of an exceptional personality.

Snuffbox with Pugs. 1752
The Neva Porcelain Factory of Dmitry Vinogradov
(1720(?)–1758), St Petersburg
Porcelain, underglaze painting, mounted with gold. 4.7 x 7.6 x 6.2 cm
(Hall 166)

A portrait of Peter the Great, the best of six mosaics from the workshop of Mikhail Lomonosov, who revived this old art form, begins the display of the era after Peter I – "the Age of Empresses". The mid-eighteenth-century reign of Empress Elizabeth saw a cultural upsurge. Works by Ivan Vishniakov, the head of the "Office of Works" painting team, the court portraitist Alexei Antropov and Count Stroganov's serf artist Ivan Argunov testify to the formation of a Russian school linked to the traditions of icon-painting and folk art. Vishniakov's portrait of Stepanida Yakovleva resembles the old parsuna, a form of depiction derived from the icon, but the techniques of Western European art give this immobile figure, in a brocade dress with either Russian or Rococo ornament, inscribed into the dark background surface an air of sensuality, freshness and secularity. This is a wedding portrait, a companion to the likeness of Mikhail, a son of the prominent St Petersburg merchant Savva Yakovlev, which also hangs here.

The Baroque, the style of Elizabeth's day, links the painting, the carved and gilded furniture, a Tula steel armchair, the costume, tapestries, glass and silverware. Particularly valuable are the first examples of Russian porcelain displayed in the next hall. Its creator, Dmitry Vinogradov, produced a snuffbox decorated with pugs using the recipe for porcelain paste that he invented and presented it to Empress Elizabeth.

By way of the large hall containing the Empress's carnival sleigh we cross to the rooms on the other side of the Dark Corridor.

The Display of Russian Culture of
the Second Half
of the 18th Century
(Hall 172)

Mina Kolokolnikov
(circa 1708 – circa 1792)
Portrait of a Young Man. 1780s
Oil on canvas. 95 x 73 cm
(Hall 163)

The former living apartments of Emperor Alexander II, decorated by Alexander Briullov, contain the display of Russian culture of the last decades of the eighteenth century, the time of Catherine II. A succession of formal and informal portraits reflects the look and faces of her reign. Nobles, ladies in waiting, favourites and distinguished cultural figures, provincial gentry, eminent merchants and the children of the imperial house crowd around portraits of the Empress herself, shown here majestically regal, there in an almost "domestic" guise. Portraiture reached a peak in the second half of the 1700s. Among likenesses that are quite often of interest only on account of the subject's name, there are very valuable works by the great masters of the time – Levitsky, Borovikovsky and Christineck or, on the contrary, by little-known Russian artists – Luzhnikov, Andreyev, Kolokolnikov, and also celebrated foreigner who worked at Catherine's court: the Swede Roslin, the Austrian Lampi. Classicism was the style of Catherine's day. Austerely majestic form and refined decoration mark the applied art on display from the first hall to the last. Palace furniture, grand porcelain and silver, articles made of steel by the craftsmen of Tula and carved ivory from Kholmogory create a eloquent picture of Russian culture in the later eighteenth century.

Casket. Late 18th century
Made by Rodion Leontyev, Tula
Blued, faceted and carved steel, with
gilded bronze and velvet lining
18.5 x 27.5 x 19.2 cm (Hall 173)

Nikolai Vereshchagin
(1770 – circa 1814)
Vase. Circa 1798
Carved and engraved walrus ivory
Height: 85 cm (Hall 173)

The open-work vase was carved from walrus ivory by an amateur craftsman, the Arkhangelsk customs official Vereshchagin, as a gift for Catherine II.
One of the best works in the collection of Tula steel is a casket made by a craftsman named Leontyev and decorated with "diamond faceting" – ornamentation where the metal is cut like gemstones, something for which the town south of Moscow was particularly famous.

The Library of Nicholas II 1894–96
Architect: Alexander Krasovsky
(Hall 178)

The Small (White) Dining Room
1894–96
Architect: Alexander Krasovsky
(Hall 188)

The Bedroom. 1838–39; 1894–95.
The Russian 19th-Century
Interiors display.
The Drawing-Room and the
Boudoir in the Empire style
Architects: Alexander Briullov;
Alexander Krasovsky (Hall 188)

From the Dark Corridor we enter the door next to the Saltykov Staircase to reach the display of the Russian Nineteenth-Century Interior, which occupies the apartments of the last Russian tsar, Nicolas II, and Empress Alexandra Fiodorovna.

Decorated very simply, like an urban apartment, in 1894–96 by the architect Alexander Krasovsky, they now provide a setting for works of applied art that in each room are linked by a common style.

Passing through the *Moderne* (Art Nouveau) interiors of the early twentieth century in former service rooms, the adjutants' and billiards rooms, we enter Nicholas II's library. It retains its architecture and carved walnut fittings stylized after the English Gothic. The built-in furniture, used here for the first time, was made in the St Petersburg factories of Melzer and Svirsky.

Beyond the library, in what was Nicholas II's study, is an interior decorated in the "Pompeian" style that formed in the early decades of the nineteenth century under the influence of the art excavated in the Ancient Roman city. The display includes items from a furniture set designed by Alexander Briullov for the lost Pompeian Dining-Room in the Winter Palace.

The adjoining rooms are the Gothic Study with furniture made by Gambs and the Boudoir in the "Second Rococo" style with furniture designed by Andrei Stakenschneider and Harald Bosse. The "drawing-rooms and boudoir of country houses in the Empire style" in the former bedroom contain furniture made from Karelian birch and poplar. Palace drawing-rooms in the same style are recreated in the former Empress's drawing-rooms that began the imperial suite.

These adjoin the main state drawing-room, the celebrated Malachite Room that was created by Alexander Briullov. Over two tonnes of the green mineral, presented to Nicholas I by the Urals mining magnate Demidov, were used to face its pilasters, columns and fireplaces. The huge malachite amphora beneath a canopy adorned this room even before the 1837 fire. The room now houses part of the world's richest collection of malachite articles, numbering around 200 items. Due to the brittle nature of the mineral it cannot be used to make large items. All the apparently solid pieces are actually thin plates skilfully arranged on a base and then carefully polished (the Russian mosaic technique). One famous exhibit – a bowl on a tripod in the form of female half-figures with goat legs standing on a malachite disk – may be the work of Western European craftsmen.

From the Malachite Room we enter the Small Dining-Room, used by Nicholas II's family for private meals. This elegant Rococo-style interior is decorated with tapestries from the St Petersburg factory – *Swans* and *Parts of the World* and has authentic furniture and china. The room is also notable because it was here, in the early hours of 26 October 1917, that the Provisional Government was arrested. This room and the Malachite Room complete the display of the "Russian Interior" and the living quarters of the Winter Palace. Next comes the enfilade of state rooms that run along the side of the palace overlooking the mighty River Neva.

The Malachite Room. 1838–39
Architect: Alexander Briullov
(Hall 189)

Bowl on a tripod in the form of winged female torsos
1809–10 (?)
Peterhof Lapidary Works (or Western Europe ?)
Malachite, ormolu. Height 134 cm; diameter 107 cm (Hall 189)

The Concert Hall. 1791–93;
830; 1837–39
Architects: Giacomo Quarenghi;
Auguste Montferrand; Vasily Stasov
(Hall 190)

The Great (Nicholas) Hall
1791–93; 1837–39
Architects: Giacomo Quarenghi;
Vasily Stasov
(Hall 191)

A. Belli
Portrait of Peter I. 1859.
Copy of the 1697 original by
Godfrey Kneller
Oil on canvas. 239.3 x 147 cm
(Hall 191)

From the Malachite Room we enter the Concert Hall from which we have a perspective view of the suite of connected halls along the Neva. The enfilade was created in 1791–93 by Giacomo Quarenghi in place of Rastrelli's planned, but unrealized five "antechambers" before the proposed immense Throne Room (in place of which the living apartments we have just left were created). The halls of the Neva Enfilade acquired their present appearance in 1838-39, when they were restored by Stasov after the fire.

The Concert Hall is decorated with grisaille painting and statues of the muses. The hall contains the shrine of Alexander Nevsky moved here in 1922 from St Petersburg's main monastery, to which Peter the Great had the relics of the sainted prince brought from Vladimir in 1724. The shrine was made in 1745–51 at the St Petersburg Mint using 1.5 tonnes of silver. The ensemble includes a pyramid, the sarcophagus carrying scenes of the Prince's famous victories – over the Swedes on the Neva in 1240, over the Livonian Order on Lake Chud in 1242 and the liberation of Pskov that same year, torchères and pedestals with compositions of arms and armour. The following Large or Nicholas Hall (it used to contain a portrait of Nicholas I) was also the Ballroom. It is the largest in the Winter Palace with a floor area of 1,103 square metres. Today it is the main hall for temporary exhibitions. Finally comes the Fore-Hall that begins the Neva Enfilade. In its centre is a rotunda with malachite columns on a stepped pedestal inlaid with coloured semi-

122

precious stones beneath a dome mounted in bronze. The rotunda was made in Livorno in 1827–34 to the order of Nikolai Demidov; the bronze elements were made in the Paris workshop of the celebrated Pierre-Philippe Thomire. From 1862 it was in the Trinity Cathedral of the Alexander Nevsky Monastery; in 1952 it was moved to the Hermitage.

A side door from the Fore-Hall leads to a gallery parallel to the Neva Enfilade. It contains a display of the Department of the History of Russian Culture reconstructing the "Romanov Gallery" that existed in the Small Hermitage until 1917, with portraits of members of the dynasty that ruled Russia for 300 years, from 1613 to 1917. The display begins with depictions of the first Romanovs, the most notable is a portrait of the young Peter I, a copy of a work now in Kensington Palace in London that was painted by Sir Godfrey Kneller in 1697, during Peter's visit to England. The parade of rulers and other Romanovs goes right up to the last tsar, Nicholas II. The gallery includes paintings recording events in the history of the dynasty – coronations, marriages and interiors of the Winter Palace. Now we return through the Neva Enfilade for a farewell glance before emerging from the Fore-Hall onto the Main Staircase of the Winter Palace, which we already know. We have come full circle, completed our route through the main complex of Hermitage buildings, visited the displays of all the museum departments and seen its most famous masterpieces. But the Hermitage is inexhaustible and always awaits you.

The Eastern (Pompeian) Gallery
(Hall 191)

The entrance to the Fore-Hall from the main (Jordan) staircase
(Hall 191)

Ilya Repin (1844–1930)
Portrait of Nicholas II. 1895
Oil on canvas
(Hall 191)

The Hermitage is located at 2, Dvortsovaya Ploshchad (Palace Square)

Transport:
Metro stations Gostiny Dvor and Nevsky Prospekt.
Bus 7 and trolley-buses 1, 7 and 10 from Nevsky Prospekt in the direction of the Admiralty spire. (Get off at the stop after Palace Square)

Opening hours
Daily, except Monday,
from 10.30 a.m. to 6.00 p.m. (5.00 p.m. on Sunday)
Last entry one hour before closing.
The entrance to the museum is through the arches from Palace Square

Besides the general displays of the main complex of the Hermitage, through which this book will guide you, the museum also includes special display facilities with separate entrances, accessible (except the General Staff) only on guided tours.

THE STATE HERMITAGE

Practical Information
The museum information desk is situated in the centre of the main vestibule.
There are computerized information stands that can give printed routes in the Jordan Gallery, in the Field Marshals' Hall and opposite the foyer of the Hermitage Theatre.

Telephone for information: +7 (812) 311 3420 and + 7 (812) 710 9079

Internet site: www.hermitagemuseum.org

Guided tours in Russian and foreign languages can be booked at the Excursion Office off the main vestibule
Advance booking by telephone: +7 (812) 571 8446

Audio guides in Russian, English, French and German are available for hire in the Jordan Gallery, ground floor (Hall 1)

For less mobile visitors
Wheelchair hire. Apply to the information desk in the main vestibule or book in advance on +7 (812) 710 9079

Computer Educational Centre
Rastrelli Gallery, ground floor (Hall 76)

Research and Education Dept. +7 (812) 710 9787, fax 312 2366

Lecture Rooms
General Staff building, 47, Naberezhnaya Reki Moiki (Moika Embankment)
Telephone: +7 (812) 710 9731

Schools Centre
Main Gallery, ground floor. Tel.: +7 (812) 110 9673

Youth Centre
General Staff building, 45, Naberezhnaya Reki Moiki (Moika Embankment)
Telephone: +7 (812) 710 9530

Centre for External Cultural and Educational Programmes. Tel. +7 (812) 710 9847

Hermitage Theatre. Administrator
Tel. +7 (812) 710 9030

Souvenir and Book stalls
Ground floor: Central cloakroom; Rastrelli gallery (souvenir shop); Commandant's entrance; near the Hall of the Kolyvan Vase
First floor: Main Staircase, upper landing; the Wooden Staircase (Halls of French Art of the 17th and 19th centuries); Main Staircase of the New Hermitage; The Knights' Hall; by the foyer of the Hermitage Theatre; Alexander Hall
Second Floor: Commandant's Staircase; Halls of French Art of the late 19th and 20th centuries (souvenir shop)

Hermitage post office. Ground floor

Café Rastrelli Gallery, ground floor

Internet Café Rastrelli Gallery, ground floor

The Treasure Galleries

A collection of works of jewellery made of gold and precious stones from ancient times to the twentieth century. There are two displays: № 1 – the "Diamond Room" (on the ground floor of the New Hermitage) and № 2 – the "Gold Room" (on the ground floor of the Winter Palace). Guided tours only. Tickets are sold at the ticket offices in the main vestibule of the Winter Palace. Groups assemble at the main control point in the Rastrelli Gallery.

Gallery № 1 – the Diamond Room. A display of jewellery: artefacts made of gold and other precious metal from Bronze Age burials, Scythian barrows, Ancient Greek necropolises and settlements in the north Black Sea coast area, northern Caucasus and southern Siberia; mediaeval Western European jewellery; Russian ecclesiastical works; the treasures of the Russian imperial court.

Gallery № 2 – the Gold Room. A display of ancient gold articles: gold from ancient burial mounds and graves in the north Black Sea coast area, Caucasus and eastern Siberia; Ancient Greek jewellery excavated in necropolises and settlements in the north Black Sea coast area; jewellery from the East.

The Winter Palace of Peter the Great

Parts of the last winter residence (personal apartments, the "Small Chambers" and grand courtyard) of the founder of St Petersburg reconstructed during restoration of the Hermitage Theatre. Guided tours only. Tickets are sold at the ticket offices in the main vestibule of the Winter Palace. Entrance from Palace Embankment below the Hermitage Theatre.

The Winter Palace of Peter the Great was constructed on land between the Neva, the Winter Canal and Millionnaya Street in several stages: 1704 – a wooden palace, the "Small Winter Chambers"; 1711 – the "Marriage Chambers", architect: Domenico Trezzini; 1716–23, the "New Winter Palace", architect: Georg Johann Mattarnovy; after 1725 – the "Newly-Built Chambers" (a square of blocks around the plot as far as Millionnaya Street), architect: Domenico Trezzini. In the 1740s the palace was placed at the disposal of the Guards (Life-Company Corps). In 1783–89, in the course of the construction of the Hermitage Theatre, the palace was dismantled and partially incorporated into the new building.

Eastern Wing of the General Staff

Displays: "Realms of the Eagle. The Empire Style" (in the authentic apartments of the Foreign Ministers of the Russian Empire Count Nesselrohde and Prince Gorchakov); "Pierre Bonnard and Maurice Denis. The decorative ensembles in the Hermitage collection" (Denis's *Story of Psyche* and Bonnard's *Mediterranean* triptych, from the mansion of the Muscovite industrialist and collector Ivan Morozov) "200 years of the Russian Foreign Ministry" (in the office, reception and secretarial rooms of the Minister of Foreign Affairs; the "Museum of the Guards". Entrance and ticket office: 6/8, Palace Square.

The building of the General Staff was constructed by the architect Carlo Rossi in the 1820s. Its wings face onto Palace Square and are linked by a triumphal arch crowned by a bronze chariot of Glory created by the sculptors Nikolai Pimenov and Vasily Demuth-Malinovsky. The eastern wing, built for the Ministries of Foreign Affairs and Finance, was transferred to the Hermitage in 1985.

The Menshikov Palace

A display of Russian culture at the time of Peter the Great (first quarter of the eighteenth century). Entrance and ticket office: 15, University Embankment, Vasilyevsky Island. Tel.: +7 (812) 323 1112

The palace of the first governor general of St Petersburg, the Most Illustrious Prince Alexander Danilovich Menshikov. Built in 1711–27 to the design of the Italian architect Giovanni Fontana; after 1713 work was supervised by Johann Gottfried Schädel. Trezzini, Carlo Bartolomeo Rastrelli, Mattarnovy and LeBlond were also involved in its construction and decoration. From 1731 the palace housed the cadet corps for the sons of nobles, after the 1917 revolution it remained a military training establishment. Transferred to the Hermitage in 1966, it was opened to the public in 1981 following restoration work. Authentic original interiors have survived in the palace.

The Museum of the Imperial Porcelain Factory

A collection of works from the Imperial Porcelain Factory dating from the eighteenth century onwards, as well as European and other Russian porcelain. Guided tours only. Entrance and ticket office: 151, Prospekt Obukhovskoi Oborony – on the premises of the Imperial Porcelain Factory (metro station: Lomonsovskaya).
Tel.: +7 (812) 326 2672

The Imperial Porcelain Factory dates back to 1744. In 1844 the porcelain museum attached to it was founded. In 2001 the museum became a department of the Hermitage. Its collection numbers over 30,000 items, with more than 600 on display.

The Staraya Derevnia Restoration and Storage Centre

An open repository: Russian and Western European furniture; the "tapestry theatre"; coaches and carriages; Eastern items (a Turkish tent); sculpture; Russian nineteenth-century painting. Guided tours only. Entrance and ticket office: 37A, Zausadebnaya Street (metro station: Staraya Derevnia).
Tel.: +7 (812) 344 9226

The first phase of the Restoration and Storage Centre complex of buildings was opened on 16 May 2003 – the Administrative, Storage, Engineering Blocks and Boilerhouse. The buildings with modern high-tech architecture are fitted with state- of- the- art systems ensuring the preservation of the articles, the functioning and aesthetics of the repository. In accordance with the General Plan of Development, by 2010 the Repository will have become one of the world's largest complexes of its kind with eight specialist blocks.

CONTENTS